How to recognize God's voice

GRAHAM FITZPATRICK

SOVEREIGN WORLD
International Edition

© Faith Builders (Publishing) Ltd 1987

International Edition
Sovereign World, P.O. Box 17, Chichester PO20 6RY

First published 1984 in the USA by
Spiritual Growth Books and edited by Richard Phillipps (Chief Editor of scan,
the ABC television magazine)

Revised UK edition first printed 1987

ISBN 0 948985 0 11

Scriptures are used by permission from following sources:

THE GOOD NEWS BIBLE – Old Testament: copyright © American
Bible Society 1976; New Testament: copyright © American Bible Society
1966, 1971, 1976.

AMPLIFIED BIBLE, Old Testament: copyright © 1962, 1964 by Zondervan
Publishing House.

Other scripture quotations from Amplified New Testament,
copyright © The Lockman Foundation 1954, 1958.

Revised Standard Version of the Bible,
copyright © 1946, 1952, 1971, 1973.

Scriptures also taken from Authorized Version of the Bible, Crown copyright.

Throughout book, some words of Scripture references are
capitalized by author for emphasis.

Dedicated to the mission field in the
Middle East, Asia, Africa, South America and Europe.

*With great appreciation to Bill Beard, Reg Scholz,
Rob Gallagher and John Kohler.*

Designed and printed for
SOVEREIGN WORLD
by Nuprint Limited, Harpenden, Herts AL5 4SE.

Contents

Bible Study Questions

INSTRUCTIONS

This book contains a number of Bible study questions at the end of each chapter. These questions are written so that any Bible study group, house meeting, cell group or other small group can have a guide for studying the Scriptures which relate to the topics discussed in this book.

Your group can study these questions a chapter at a time or in any other amount.

Trust the Lord to reveal the answers to these questions. This book is not your textbook. The Bible is your textbook and source of truth.

1

The Holy Bible

Being able to recognize how God speaks, is a crucial thing for every human to know. There are a number of ways in which God speaks.

The most important and only infallible way that God speaks to people is through the Holy Bible. Even though the writers of the Bible were not infallible, the inspired words and teachings of the Bible, the Holy Scriptures, are.

The Bible to the Christian is the Word of God. It is God communicating His thoughts to you through the printed page. If you wish to know what God thinks on a given issue, seek the answer in the words of the Holy Scriptures.

Only totally true and reliable source

God has, through the inspired words of the Scriptures, revealed that the Bible is the only totally true and reliable source of knowing God's thoughts. Read what 2 Timothy 3:16 says:

> **Every Scripture is God-breathed – given by His inspiration – and is profitable for instruction, for reproof and conviction of sin, for correction of error and discipline in obedience, and for training in righteousness.**
> *Amplified Version*

If you want to know and live God's will, you must have your thoughts, purposes and actions filled with and obedient to the teachings of God's Holy Scriptures. Joshua 1:8 says you should meditate every day on the Holy Scriptures.

No book other than the Bible contains total truth from God. The Hindu writings, Buddha's teachings, the Book of Mormon and other religions' written teachings (though they contain some noble aims such as helping other people) were not inspired by God. They are human opinions about God. The Bible is God's revelation of Himself through the writings of the Prophets, Apostles and other writers of the Old and New Testaments.

Some churchgoing people don't give the Holy Scriptures a high place of importance in their lives. They argue that the Scriptures are no more important than the writings of theologians or philosophers and the books of other religions.

This is wrong. Jesus and the Apostles never relied on the teachings of theologians or philosophers or the religious experiences of other persons as the authority and basis of their teachings.

Bible as the final authority

It is clear in the New Testament that Jesus and the Apostles constantly quoted the Old Testament Scriptures as their source of authority and teaching. Read the Gospels and the Book of Acts and see how many times Jesus and the Apostles quote the Old Testament Scriptures. The Apostles also regarded every word of Jesus as later recorded in the New Testament as being the Word of God.

Look at Jesus' words about the importance of the Scriptures. He said in Matthew 5:17–18:

> **Do not think that I have come to do away with the law of Moses and the teachings of the prophets. I have not come to do away with them, but to make their teachings come true. Remember that as long as heaven and earth last, not the least point nor the smallest detail of the law will be done away with – not until the end of all things.**
> *Good News Version*

6

In the above, 'the law of Moses and the teachings of the prophets' means the Old Testament taken as a whole. Jesus also spoke of the importance of the Holy Scriptures when He said in John 10:35:

> ...and the Scripture cannot be set aside or cancelled or broken or annulled....
> *Amplified Version*

Jesus stated forcefully that if a man-made religious opinion or theory or teaching conflicted with the teachings of the Holy Scriptures, then this religious opinion or teaching was wrong. Mark 7:5–8 says:

> And the Pharisees and scribes kept asking (Jesus), Why do your disciples not order their way of living according to the tradition handed down by the forefathers to be observed, but eat with hands unwashed and ceremonially not purified? But he said to them, Excellently and truly – so that there will be no room for blame – did Isaiah prophesy of you, the pretenders and hypocrites, as it stands written: This people (constantly) honor Me with their lips, but their heart holds itself off and is far distant from Me. In vain – fruitlessly and without profit – do they worship Me, ordering and teaching to be obeyed as doctrines the commandments and precepts of men. You disregard and give up and bid depart from you the commandment of God, and cling to the tradition of men – keeping it carefully and faithfully.
> *Amplified Version*

Paul's attitude

The Apostle Paul's words also reveal how everyone should regard the Holy Bible. He said in Romans 15:4:

> For whatever was thus written in former days was written for our instruction, that by (our steadfast and patient) endurance and the encouragement (drawn) from the Scriptures, we might hold fast and cherish hope.
> *Amplified Version*

Paul's actions show that he used the Scriptures as his

source of doctrine and teachings. Acts 17:2–3 says:

> **According to his usual habit, Paul went to the synagogue.
> There during three Sabbaths, he held discussions with
> the people, quoting and explaining the Scriptures and
> proving from them that the Messiah had to suffer and
> rise from death.**
> *Good News Version*

From this historical record, it is clear that the Apostle
Paul did not quote as his source of authority and teaching
the words of such philosophers as the Greeks Plato or
Aristotle, or religious leaders of the previous era such as
the Pharisees Hillel and Shummai (who were highly
regarded by many religious Jews).

Instead, Paul quoted the words and teachings of the
Old Testament and the words and teachings of Jesus
which were later to be recorded in the New Testament, as
his final and only infallible source of authority in deciding
which religious teachings were from God and which were
not.

Look how strictly Paul stuck to the Scriptures as his
final authority in deciding which religious teachings were
from God and which were merely human opinion! Paul
even corrected the other Apostles if they followed any
man-made religious teaching in preference to the teachings
of the Old Testament and Jesus on the matter. Paul writes
in Galatians 2:11–13 about when he was at Antioch with
the Apostle Peter:

> **But when Peter came to Antioch, I opposed him in
> public, because he was clearly wrong. Before some men
> who had been sent by James arrived there, Peter had
> been eating with the Gentile brothers. But after these
> men arrived, he drew back and would not eat with the
> Gentiles, because he was afraid of those who were in
> favour of circumcising them. The other Jewish brothers
> also started acting like cowards along with Peter; and
> even Barnabas was swept along by their cowardly action.**
> *Good News Version*

Here Peter was following the man-made religious teaching of some Jewish Christians who foolishly mixed Biblical teaching with Pharisee tradition. This tradition stated that no Jew should enter or eat in the house of a non-Jew. This teaching was not sanctioned by the Old Testament or Jesus, so Paul chastised Peter about it. Acts 10:1–48 shows that God also had previously given Peter a vision which revealed that he should not separate himself in this way from his non-Jewish Christian friends.

Sadly at present, some silly church leaders rank pagan philosophers and other religious leaders with the Holy Bible in deciding what religious teaching is agreed to by God. They follow whatever is the fashionable philosophy in universities and theological colleges, even if these teachings disagree with the teachings of Jesus, the Prophets, Apostles and other writers of the Holy Scriptures. Paul said in 1 Corinthians 3:18–20:

> **Let no person deceive himself. If any one among you supposes that he is wise in this age – let him discard his (worldly) discernment and recognize himself as dull, stupid and foolish, without (true) learning and scholarship; let him become a fool that he may become (really) wise. For this world's wisdom is foolishness – absurdity and stupidity – with God. For it is written, He lays hold of the wise in their (own) craftiness. And again, the Lord knows the thoughts and reasonings of the (humanly) wise and recognizes how futile they are.**
> *Amplified Version*

Acts 17:28 records that Paul did quote in his preaching at least once the words of some Greek poets. But he didn't use the words of these poets as a source of authority for his teaching and preaching. He just used the poets' words as an illustration in his preaching to the Athenians of something that the Scriptures already taught. Paul did not quote poets or other so-called great people if their words were different from what the Old Testament or Jesus taught.

Unconditional obedience to leaders?

Paul's actions show that he would not listen to the teachings of the highest religious leader in the country, if that leader was teaching and acting in a way that was contrary to the teachings of the Holy Scriptures. See Paul's reaction to the Jewish High Priest (see Acts 23:1–5).

The office of the High Priest had been set up by God in the time of Moses (see Leviticus 21:10–15 and Exodus 28:1–30). God had made the position of High Priest to be the highest or second highest (after Moses and his successors) or equal highest (with Moses) religious authority in ancient Israel. But the High Priests in Jesus' time and in Paul's time rejected many of the teachings of the Scriptures that related to Jesus, rejected Jesus Himself and refused to be born again of God the Holy Spirit (Matthew 26:3–4), 57–68, Acts 5:17–18, 27–33, Acts 13:26–34 and Romans 8:9). So Paul rejected their religious authority and taught others to do likewise. In Acts 23:3, Paul calls the highest religious leader in Israel 'a whitewashed wall', a hypocrite.

Paul ignored the teachings of the philosophers, the Jewish High Priest and other religious leaders:

> So they set a date with Paul, and a large number of them came that day to the place where Paul was staying. From morning until night he explained to them his message about the Kingdom of God, and he tried to convince them about Jesus by quoting from the Law of Moses and the writings of the prophets.
> *Acts 28:23, Good News Version*

While preaching in Rome, Paul used the Scriptures as his sole authority for what he was teaching. It is such a pity that so many church leaders in the following centuries didn't follow Paul's example.

The apostle Peter

Peter also had the highest regard for the Scriptures. In 2 Peter 1:20–21 he writes:

(Yet) first (you must) understand this, that no prophecy of Scripture is (a matter) of any personal or private or special interpretation (loosening, solving). For no prophecy ever originated because some man willed it (to do so) – it never came by human impulse – but as men spoke from God who were borne along (moved and impelled) by the Holy Spirit.
Amplified Version

Peter saw the words of the Old Testament and of the New Testament as being the final authority in deciding which religious teachings are correct and which are not.

Jesus strongly rebuked Peter

On the recorded occasions where Peter mistakenly tried to suggest or do something which was not in agreement with the teachings of the Holy Scriptures, he was corrected.

The first of these was where Peter tried to convince Jesus not to want to suffer and die (see Mark 8:31–33). Jesus strongly rebuked Peter for wanting Him to do things which were in disobedience to the predictions of the Old Testament prophets. The second of these occasions relates to his encounter with Paul at Antioch that has already been discussed. Peter must have learnt his lesson after being rebuked on these two occasions. This is because Peter's later teachings show that he changed his wrong attitudes after being shown the truth (see 1 Peter and 2 Peter).

Peter taught that Paul's writings to the early churches were Scriptures. 2 Peter 3:15–16 says:

Look on our Lord's patience as the opportunity he is giving you to be saved, just as our dear brother Paul wrote to you, using all the wisdom that God gave him. This is what he says in all of his letters when he writes on the subject. There are some difficult things in his letters which ignorant and unstable people explain falsely, as they do with other passages of the scriptures.
Good News Version

Peter didn't say here that Paul's preserved letters to the Colossians, Ephesians, Romans and other churches were just Paul's own personal opinion. Instead, Peter stated that these writings of Paul were all part of the Holy Scriptures. Therefore, the Apostle Peter regarded Paul's letters to the churches as being wholly inspired by God. Sadly, some present-day church leaders have the opposite attitude to Peter's. They foolishly believe part of Paul's writings in the Bible and parts of the writings of other authors of the Bible were only their own personal opinions.

Do not waste time

In later chapters, you will learn how the Spirit of Jesus uses other ways of speaking to Christians. Remember, when reading these later chapters, that if the Holy Bible already reveals God's will about a particular question, then you show little faith in God and/or ignorance, if you then look for special revelations from God the Holy Spirit about the same topic.

For example, don't waste time seeking to have God give an inner voice of His Holy Spirit on whether to have sex outside of marriage. The Bible already gives the answer. You should always look to the Bible first to seek God's thoughts about any matter.

Experiences only used as examples

Other chapters in this book quote spiritual experiences – showing how God speaks to people by His Holy Spirit. These experiences are not quoted as an authority or basis of teaching and doctrine. Only the Holy Scriptures can be used as a Christian's authority for what he believes and teaches.

The main things in this book are the Scriptures which are quoted and the explanations of these Scriptures that are given. The experiences or testimonies quoted which related to the writer are given only as modern-day examples of things which the Holy Bible already teaches.

It is important to experience God and His love, power, forgiveness, cleansing and other miracles. It is not sufficient to only mentally know all of the correct doctrines of Christianity. Even though God is a God of Truth (see 1 John 5:7, John 14:6), He is also a God Who commands us to know Him in our daily experience of life. Ephesians 3:19 shows this:

> **(That you may really come) to know practically – through experience for yourselves – the love of Christ, which far surpasses mere knowledge (without experience); that you may be filled (through all your being) unto all the fullness of God – (that is) may have the richest measure of the divine Presence and become a body wholly filled and flooded with God Himself.**
> *Amplified Version*

However, we cannot form our doctrines on the basis of our varying human spiritual experiences. This is because even some godly Christians over the centuries were deceived by some spiritual experiences which suggested things contrary to the Holy Scriptures. God has provided the Bible as the final judge of what is true doctrine.

This book wishes to encourage you to have always scripture-based teachings in your mind. Do not fall for the trap of forming your beliefs merely on the basis of your own spiritual experiences, the writer's spiritual experiences or any other person's spiritual experiences, no matter how holy or dedicated to God the person may seem to be.

Chapter 1   The Holy Bible

1 Is the Holy Scriptures the most important way that God speaks to us? If so, why?
2 Is the Scriptures a record of human opinions about God? Or are they God's revelation of Himself to humans?
3 If the writers of the Bible were not perfect in their grammar or their style of writing, does this mean that God did not reveal to them the truths that they wrote?

4 What was the Jesus' attitude to the Scriptures?

5 What was Paul's and Peter's attitude to the Scriptures?

6 Was Paul right in correcting Peter's attitude in the incident spoken of in Galatians 2:11–14?

7 If a great religious leader teaches something different from the Bible, who should we believe—the Bible or him/her?

8 Should we seek to have the Spirit of Jesus give us a revelation of His will, if the Scriptures already show what His will is?

9 Can we base our teachings and doctrines on our own spiritual experiences and other people's experiences of God's power, love, miracles and presence?

10 What are the advantages of God recording His thoughts and His will in a book?

2

The intimate ways that God speaks

The Holy Bible is the most important way in which God speaks to us, as Chapter 1 explains. It is the *only* infallible source of guidance from God. It is far superior and less open to human error than the three other main ways that God speaks to us. These are:

1 The inner witness of God the Holy Spirit
2 The 'still small voice' or inner voice of God the Holy Spirit, and
3 Signs in our circumstances.

These three ways that God speaks are provided by Him only because there are in everyone's life some situations for which the Bible does not give a specific answer.

The Scriptures do not tell you, for example, whether you should live in France, Greece, Lebanon, China or any other country. They do not state whether you should live in the city or on a farm, or whether you should work for the post office or in a trade, or as a doctor or in some other vocation. The Bible does not tell whether to become a boss at work or not. It does not explain to women whom they should pick as their marriage partner – whether to marry John or Paul or Fred or Sam, or not to get married at all. God does not tell men whether to marry Pam or Mary or Sue, or stay single. The Bible does not explain how you should invest any money you might have, whether to buy a block of land or invest in an oil company or buy a business. In fact, the Bible does not make a rule that you should invest your money. The Bible does not say whether God wants you to pray for this miracle or that miracle, or whether God wants you to be a teacher or a counsellor or a leader in your local church. The Bible does not say whether God wants you to risk your life by taking Bibles into communist or Muslim countries or not, or whether you should get married on this date or another date, or whether to buy this car or one of the many other cars on the market, or to play football or baseball or run as a means of keeping your body healthy – or whether He wants you to avoid competition sport this year.

it is necessary to study the Bible to understand the less important (but definitely not unimportant) ways in which God desires to speak to humans. The following chapters will present this study.

God never speaks against what he has written

Right from the start, know clearly that the Spirit of Jesus will never give you an inner witness or 'still small voice' or a sign that will suggest that God is saying something to you contrary to the teachings of His Scriptures. He will never ever do this. Remember this while studying the following chapters.

There are too many Christians these days claiming that the Holy Spirit has told them to do something, when He has not.

We cannot earn guidance

The following chapters show that praying a lot, praising God and doing other things will make one more receptive to the voice of God. But the writer is not suggesting that by prayer and praise, Christians can force God to speak to them or that they can earn an answer from Him. We cannot force God to speak to us. Nor can we ever make ourselves worthy enough by our praying, praising and other efforts, for God to feel obliged to speak to us.

God wishes to speak to us not because we are good enough, but because He loves us and because through the death and resurrection of Jesus Christ, He wishes to form a personal love-trust relationship with every one of us.

God can speak at any time He likes. However, by praying more and practising some of the other Biblical principles in this book, we can open our thoughts to the Spirit of Jesus when He is trying to communicate with us. Remember this when reading the chapter 'Improving Your Ability to Recognize God's Voice' and other parts of this teaching book.

Picking God's voice from evil spirits

Learn to recognize God the Holy Spirit's guidance from the things which come from Satanic spirits, and from your own human imagination and human thoughts. God desires for you to know His voice. Listen for God's voice, or you will never be able to walk closely with God in obedience and faith. There will always be something lacking in your Christian life.

Some Christians know how important it is to obey the teachings of the Scriptures. But they know little of obedience to Jesus Christ through the day-to-day guidance of God the Holy Spirit. Some Christians do this in ignorance because they have never been taught how to tell the difference between things which come from God the Holy Spirit and those which come from demons or the human imagination.

Other Christians do not like the idea of getting day-by-day guidance from God the Holy Spirit because it frightens them. Fear is a lack of faith, as Matthew 14:30–31 explains. Others don't really want to be guided by God's Spirit because they prefer to let God run only a certain part of their lives.

You don't have to pray every minute of every day to

hear God's voice. However, unless you are prepared to spend an hour or more of every day in prayer, it will be hard for you to recognize the leadings of God the Holy Spirit very much.

God can speak when you are not praying

God can try to speak to you at times when you are not praying. For example, God spoke to Moses in the wilderness of Midian at a time when Moses was not in prayer (see Exodus 3:1–4). In 1 Samuel 3:1–9, God tried to communicate with Samuel even though Samuel was not praying at the time – in fact, Samuel thought it was his master Eli calling.

God can speak to you at any time. But if you are praying, you are more likely to be in a mental state receptive to God's voice.

You cannot be too busy for God

Do you say that you are too busy to talk to God, and listen to Him a lot? Then you must be wasting time on less important things.

The strongest Christians of all denominations over the centuries have been men and women who have spent an hour or more each day waiting on God in prayer and in praying short one-minute or so prayers on and off through the rest of the day. As a result, these Christians became very receptive to the Spirit of Jesus. Look at the lives of such people as Wesley, Finney, Moody and Whitefield, to name a few.

An intensely personal love for God

Do not seek to recognize God's voice more easily just so you can find solutions to your problems. God wishes you to know His will and to give you solutions to your problems. But the main reason that he wants you to become more attuned to His voice, which speaks through the Scriptures and the inward guidance of the Holy Spirit, is so that you can deepen the intensity of your personal love relationship to Him.

It is important to also relate to God in a group situation, where believers meet together for teaching, prayer, praise, holy communion and friendship. This is seen in Hebrews 10:25, Acts 2:46–47 and 5:42. However, this relating to God in group situations is not sufficient in itself. A strong personal friendship – love relationship to God is also greatly emphasised in His teachings in the Holy Scriptures.

Some people try to do without a group relationship to God. Others underemphasise an intensely personal relationship to Him. Every person needs both of these.

The greatest times of finding more knowledge of God's will for your life are usually those times when you seek to commune more deeply with Him and grow in your love for Him.

Psalm 34:10 says:

> **The young lions lack food and suffer hunger, but they that seek (inquire of and require) the Lord (by right of their need and on authority of His Word), none of them shall lack any beneficial thing.**
> *Amplified Version*

To the writer, 'Any beneficial thing' includes hearing God's voice and knowing God's will. Psalm 105:4 also speaks of seeking to know God more closely and personally than anyone else. It says:

> **Seek, inquire of and for the Lord, and crave Him and His strength (His might and inflexibility to temptation, seek and require His face and His presence continually) evermore.**
> *Amplified Version*

The more that you know God in an intensely personal way, the more that you will be able to recognize His Spirit's voice.

Other key points

Of course, it is not necessary to pray specifically about all the little, routine decisions you make in the course of a busy day – when to eat, when to brush one's hair, when to bathe or shower. For the answer to this, see Chapter 15.

A final point: It is vitally important to understand and practice the Scriptural principles which relate to God speaking to you through the inner witness, the still small voice and circumstances, for two reasons. Firstly, a personal relationship to God must involve two-way communication about each area of your life. Secondly, there are too many people nowadays claiming that God has spoken to them, when it is really only their own imagination, own emotions or demonic spirits speaking to them.

If we wait patiently for God to speak to us, He will direct our path and speak to us about many things.

Chapter 2 The intimate ways that God speaks

1 Are the inner witness, the 'still small' voice and signs in our circumstances open to human error in their recognition?
2 Would God ever give you guidance by His Spirit that is contrary to the teachings of the Scriptures?
3 Does praying, praising, fasting and other similar things earn an answer from God when you are seeking to know His will? If not, what is the use of these things?
4 What are reasons why some Christians would not necessarily wish to hear God speak regularly to them by His Spirit?
5 What is the main reason that God wishes for you to be able to recognize His voice more easily?

3

The inner witness of the Holy Spirit

The inner witness is one of the major ways God guides us. Romans 8:16 says of this:

> **The Spirit itself (Himself) beareth witness with our spirit, that we are the children of God.**
> *Authorised Version*

This verse in its specific context refers to the Spirit of God giving Christians a witness or spiritual assurance or spiritual feeling in their spirit which reveals to their mind that they are children of God. It also infers that God speaks to Christians by giving them an inner witness in their spirit about other matters.

Proverbs 20:27 teaches in part that God speaks to us through our spirit:

> **The spirit of man is the candle of the Lord, searching all the inward parts of the belly.**
> *Authorised Version*

If our spirit is the candle of the Lord, God gives us enlightenment and understanding of Himself through our spirit.

Here is one definition of the inner witness: the way in *def'n* which you as a Christian, seeking God's will in prayer (and sometimes when you are not praying), have the Holy

Spirit communicate spiritual feelings to your own human spirit. This then reveals God's will to your mind.

The inner witness can also be defined as where God the Holy Spirit gives you a peace or a joy in your human spirit, when you are doing or mentally picturing doing something which is God's will. It is also a lack of peace or a horrible uneasy feeling in your spirit, when you are doing or thinking of doing something which is not God's will.

Sometimes, you have to wait a little while to get quiet enough in mind and spirit to recognize this type of guidance. The inner witness is also spoken of in Philippians 4:7:

And God's peace which is far beyond human understanding, will keep your hearts and minds safe in Christ Jesus.
Good News Version

inner peace as a guide

This verse explains firstly, that your human mind won't be able to understand fully the inner witness of peace from God. Secondly, it shows that this inner peace will act as a guide to your heart and mind to keep you safe in the will of Jesus Christ.

Colossians 3:15 relates to the fact that if you don't relate to other people with the unselfish loving attitudes expressed in Colossians 3:5–14, you will not have peace in your spirit, mind and body. It also suggests that you should let the inner witness of peace from God the Son rule the decisions you are going to make in your life. It says:

The peace that Christ gives is to guide you in the decisions that you make.
Good News Version

Note that Philippians 4:7 uses the words 'God's peace' and Colossians 3:15 uses the words 'the peace that Christ gives'. This peace is therefore not from the human emotions but is from the Spirit of Jesus.

Too often people think that the witness that Romans

8:16 talks about is a physical something. It is not. It is a spiritual something. It is the Spirit of God bearing witness with our spirits. He does not bear witness with our bodies.

You cannot go by physical feeling. The inner witness type of guidance of the Holy Spirit is a thing that you sense, not in your physical body and not in your emotions. The inner witness has nothing to do with physical feelings. The inner witness has to do with spiritual feelings within your spirit. It will sometimes take a Christian many years of prayer and practise before he can tell the difference between these two things.

Ask God's forgiveness when you mistake your own physical feelings for the inner witness spiritual feelings in your spirit. Then praise Him for the times when you truly recognize the guidance of Jesus Christ through an inner witness.

Romans 8:16 shows that the inner witness of the Holy Spirit is a feeling in your human spirit:

The Spirit (Himself) bears witness with our spirit.
Amplified Version

It doesn't say, 'The Spirit bears witness with your physical body' or 'The Spirit bears witness with your physical feelings', does it? If you are going to learn to be led by God, you must learn to know the difference between feelings in your physical emotions and body, and feelings in your spirit.

You will possibly make mistakes while you are learning. You will possibly mistake an emotional desire or feeling to do something for the inner witness of the Holy Spirit in your spirit. But just because some people make mistakes in learning to recognize the inner witness, don't 'throw the baby out with the bath water'. Some Christians have wrongly thrown away the value of being led by the inner witness because people make mistakes in recognizing it.

Paul, Peter, John and many other dedicated Christians learnt how to allow the inner witness to be one, but not the only, means by which Jesus guided them. We should follow their example.

Chapter 3   What is the inner witness of the Holy Spirit

1 How many Scriptures can you find which talk about the inner witness?
2 What does Romans 8:16 infer about the inner witness?
3 Which verses in the Bible suggest that the inner witness is not a human emotion, but is a fruit of the Holy Spirit?
4 What things does Philippians 4:7 teach about the inner witness?

This author has read books which speak against the idea that God also speaks by the inner witness or the 'still small voice' (discussed in later chapters). The problem with these books is that they are written by people who twist the Scriptures to fit in with their own *personal* experiences.

Their experience of life tells them that God doesn't speak in these ways. Therefore, they then write books to try to prove that the Scriptures do not say that God speaks in these ways.

These writers accuse others of over-emphasizing experiences, while they themselves are ruled by their own experiences more than most others.

4

More about the inner witness

The inner witness involves a number of important things.

Only born-again Christians can have inner witnesses of God the Holy Spirit in their own spirit. Unbelievers are not sons and daughters of God. They do not have the Holy Spirit living in them. Therefore, they cannot have inner witnesses from Him. Romans 8:14 says:

For all who are led by the Spirit of God are sons of God.
Amplified Version

Unbelievers are not led by the Holy Spirit, even though unbelievers are convicted of their sins by Him (see John 16:8). It would be dangerous for an unbeliever to follow the leadings in his spirit. This is because his spirit is not joined to the Holy Spirit and will often tell him to do evil.

When you are born again, your human spirit and the Holy Spirit become one with one another. 1 Corinthians 6:17 says:

But the person who is united to the Lord becomes one spirit with him.
Amplified Version

Refer also to John 17:21–23.

Therefore, since your spirit becomes one with the Holy Spirit, your human spirit can very easily find God's will.

One of the two forms that the inner witness of the Holy Spirit takes (the other is discussed in Chapter 5) is a peace and a joy in your spirit when you are praying and/or thinking about doing a certain thing. This peace and joy is God's way of telling you to do the thing that you are thinking of doing.

The inner witness is the presence of the fruit of the Holy Spirit spoken of in Galatians 5:22. Two of these fruits are peace and joy. These are not human emotions of peace and joy in your body or physical emotions. Instead, they are fruit of the Holy Spirit in your spirit.

Galatians 5:22 also refers to the sort of fruit or character that will be seen in the life of a person who is God-controlled. This verse defines the character of the Holy Spirit. It also infers that two of these fruits of the Holy Spirit, peace and joy, will be used by God to guide a Christian in what is God's will, so that he can be God-controlled.

A personal example

When God has given me an inner witness in my spirit that it is His will for me to do something, my spirit felt incredible feelings of joy or peace flooding it. These were not in my body or emotions. Here is a personal example:

One night at a church prayer meeting, a great peace came into my spirit, guiding me to pray for a person with whom I was working at the time. I obeyed this inner witness of the Holy Spirit in my heart. I prayed for an hour or so at the meeting, asking God's Spirit to reveal to this person the need of Him.

I finished interceding and had an inner witness of joy that God was going to do as I had asked. The next day at work, this person came to me and expressed a desire to talk to a minister and had began at 7.30 p.m. the previous night (exactly at the time I began praying) to think about what was going to happen after death. After then, this person wouldn't stop talking about God with friends for the rest of the night. They were at a nightclub.

Note that I had never spoken to this person about God before. This person experienced exactly what the inner witness of the Holy Spirit led me to pray about. The miracle occurred in the person's life exactly the same time that God, through the inner witness, had me begin to pray.

Such a thing couldn't have been a coincidence. There would be one chance in a million of such a thing happening without a miracle.

Other keys

God can speak to you when you are not praying, praising, expressing love to Him and telling Him that you will do whatever He says. However, when you are doing these things, it is less likely that your own human feelings will arise in you. This is not a rule that applies to all situations though. It is merely a guide.

The inner witness, instead of human feelings, are more likely to be present at these times, because these practises encourage you to be more Holy Spirit-controlled.

Another key point to note about the inner witness is this: An inner witness of the Holy Spirit in one's spirit will never disagree with Bible principles. This is because the Word and the Spirit of God never disagree.

For example, if a woman said that she had an inner witness of the Holy Spirit in her human spirit to never forgive her husband for being nasty, this is obviously not a true inner witness from God. This is because this so-called inner witness is suggesting something which is the opposite of Biblical teaching.

Each inner witness must be checked to see if it agrees with Scripture.

Chapter 4   More about the inner witness

1 Why can only a born-again Christian have an inner witness of the Holy Spirit?
2 Galatians 5:22 does not only relate to getting guidance from God. However, what does it indicate about God speaking by the inner witness?

5

An uneasy spirit

Not only does the inner witness of the Holy Spirit operate by God giving you peace and/or joy in your spirit when you think about doing something He wants you to do. The inner witness also operates by God's Spirit giving you an uneasy, tight, horrible feeling in your spirit, when your mind is mentally picturing doing something that is not His will.

The inner witness is not only given by God as a means of showing you what is His will. It is also given to you as a way of showing you what is not His will.

The Spirit of Jesus will give you an inner witness of uneasiness and tightness in your spirit, if you are thinking of disobeying any of the teachings of the Holy Scriptures. For example, if you are thinking of stealing pens and paper from your workplace, the Holy Spirit will automatically give you an inner witness not to do this.

Similarly, if you are considering being immoral with someone, the Holy Spirit will automatically give you an inner witness of a lack of peace to tell you not to do this.

The Holy Spirit will also give you this uneasiness and tightness in your spirit about things not specifically mentioned in Scripture. For example, sometime when I've eaten enough during a day, I have a tight uneasy feeling in my spirit from God's Spirit if I go to the fridge to eat some more. Or if I have not eaten enough, the reverse happens.

The more sensitive you become to God's Spirit within,

the more you will be amazed how many times during the day you will have a peace about doing some course of action or you will have an unpleasant horrible tightness in your spirit about doing some other thing.

When I've been seeking to find God's will in hours of prayer about a particular matter, very often the following has occurred. God has given me an inner witness not to take certain actions relating to my job, my relatives, my friends and my activities at my local church.

These inner witnesses proved to be truly from God. This is because of the results which, in the long run, occurred from obeying them. Also, they were not contrary to Scripture.

The Spirit of God will not give you an inner witness about everything that you are to do each day. But you will be surprised about the number of things that He is trying to guide you about, if you train yourself to become sensitive to Him speaking to you in this way.

God doesn't want to make us robots. However, He does want to constantly help us remain in *His perfect plan* for our lives (a) by giving us inner witnesses of peace about what is His will for us; and (b) by giving us inner witnesses of uneasiness in our spirits when He sees us thinking about disobeying.

God uses most importantly the Holy Scriptures and then the inner witness and the inner voice from His Spirit to guide us, just as a bird covers and protects its babies with its wings.

Illustrations

A few other illustrations of what the inner witness of the Holy Spirit is are as follows:

1   If you are asking God in prayer whether you are meant to be a church leader, and you then get a great joy and peace in your spirit (not in your human emotions), this is the inner witness of God telling you to become one.

29

2　If, while asking God in the name of Jesus whether He wants you to get a job at Mr Jones' law office and you get a great peace and joy in your spirit, this is the inner witness of the Holy Spirit telling you that He wants you to work there.

3　After spending time seeking God's will about whether you should pray for your brother, who has just died of a heart attack in front of you, to rise from the dead, His Spirit gives you great peace and joy while you are thinking of doing this. This means that God will raise him from the dead if you pray in faith and certainty. This example doesn't refer to where a person, without beforehand seeking to know God's will about the matter, decides to try to raise someone from the dead.

4　If you are praying about marrying someone and you have a terrible feeling of uneasiness and lack of joy in your spirit (even if you have peace in your emotions about marrying), God is saying not to marry this person. I know someone who disobeyed this inner witness of uneasiness and a lack of joy in her spirit and ended up divorced.

Chapter 5　An uneasy spirit

1　What are the different sorts of feelings the Holy Spirit gives Christians in their spirits to guide them?

2　Why would the Holy Spirit give you an inner witness of lack of peace or uneasiness, if you were considering disobeying one of the teachings of the Scriptures?

6

Physical feelings and inner witness

I stress again that the inner witness of peace and/or joy from God the Holy Spirit is not the same as emotionally feeling good about doing something. In many cases, the inner witness of God's Spirit in your human spirit will tell you to do things which are the opposite of how you feel in your natural feelings or emotions about the same matters.

For example, when a person hurts a Christian woman, she may feel angry, rejected and wounded in her human feelings. However, in her human spirit, God the Holy Spirit will be giving her an inner witness of peace and joy to guide her to forgive and love this person who has hurt her.

Again, a Christian man may feel very peaceful and joyful in his physical feelings about buying a new car. However, in his human spirit, he may at the same time have an inner witness of lack of peace or uneasiness from God the Holy Spirit. God may be giving him this lack of peace because He may know that the money that would be spent on the new car is needed for some other more useful purpose soon. God has a perfect plan for everything that we may do.

Christians should not do what their human emotions tell them to do. Their human emotions are not an infallible guide of right and wrong. For human emotions, even in the lives of Christians, can be full of anger, resentment, fear, hurt, loneliness, depression and other sinful things.

As a Christian you are tempted greatly to get out of God's will, if you decide what you should do day by day, on the basis of how you feel emotionally about each course of action. Instead of following what your feelings or emotions tell you to do, firstly, God wants you to do whatever the Bible teaches about the matter.

Secondly, He wants you to do whatever the inner witness or inner voice of His Spirit guides you to do.

Some Christians do not understand what the Word of God teaches about their spirit. For some Christians easily mistake what they feel in their physical feelings or emotions as being the same as an inner witness of God's Spirit in their spirit. This sort of Christian says, 'I've got a peace in my heart about marrying that person'. However, they fail to realise that the peace that they have in themselves is not in their spirit, but is only in their emotions.

Your human emotions originate in the physical brain in your head. These feelings originate in the emotional centres in your brain and are transferred to your body by the autonomic nervous system. The inner witness of God the Holy Spirit does not originate in the emotional centres of your physical brain but in your non-physical non-material spirit.

Your spirit spiritually feels the inner witness of peace and joy from God the Holy Spirit. Your spirit does not *feel* the inner witness physically. The inner witness is not something that you feel in your brain or in your body,

However, God has made you so that when your spirit is spiritually feeling an inner witness of peace and/or joy, your human mind will be aware of this fact. Once you enter these realms in Jesus' name, you will understand. Your human spirit somehow lets your physical brain be aware of the spiritual feelings from God the Holy Spirit that are occurring in your spirit at this time.

You must be very clear in your understanding of the difference between your physical emotions' feelings and the spiritual feelings in your spirit. It often takes many hours of waiting on God in prayer where you praise and thank Him, committing yourself to do whatever He tells you (see Romans 12:1–2), and praying in the Spirit, before you will be able to recognize the difference between the two. But as already stated, God can also give you an inner witness when you are not praying.

If you say that you have a peace in yourself about doing some course of action (e.g. changing your job), seek to find out whether this peace is really in your human spirit or not. This will help you to become more sensitive to God's guidance. If you really trust Him to, God will teach you the difference between the inner witness and feelings of peace and/or joy which are only physical feelings.

Objective scriptural principles

Many ask, 'How can I know the difference between my own emotions and the inner witness of the Holy Spirit?' The answer: Any feeling that you think is an inner witness will not be from Him unless it is in agreement with the objective principles of the Holy Scriptures such as:

> **So whether you eat or drink, or whatever you do, do all to the glory of God.**
> *1 Corinthians 10:31 RSV*

A feeling will not be an inner witness of the Holy Spirit if it is leading you to do something which does not in some way bring glory to God. Doing everything for the glory of God means thinking, speaking and doing everything in your life in such a way that it encourages others or yourself to honour and value God above everyone and everything else.

> **But seek ye first the kingdom of God, and his righteousness; and all these things shall be added unto you.**
> *Matthew 6:33 – Authorized Version*

The kingdom of God relates to God's rule in heaven and the spiritual world (see 2 Timothy 4:18), but it also relates to His rule over your human spirit, mind and body (see Luke 17:20–21) and over the daily activities of your life (see Matthew 7:21).

A feeling will not be an inner witness of God unless it guides you into allowing Him to rule over some part of your daily thoughts, feelings and actions. If it is encouraging you to be self-reliant, self-centred or proud or it is encouraging others to focus more attention and love on you or some other person or thing than on Jesus, then this feeling is not an inner witness.

The Scriptures command you to help your Christian brothers and sisters in both spiritual and natural things (see Hebrews 10:24, Philippians 2:4) and help your non-Christian family members or associates to turn to the Lord Jesus (see Matthew 28:19–20). A feeling cannot be from God if it leads you to do something contrary to this.

There are other important Scriptural principles which could be added to the above list.

7

The inner voice of the Holy Spirit

The third most usual way God speaks to Christians is through an inner voice. The Holy Scriptures is the main, the most usual, source of guidance. The inner witness of God's Spirit is the second most important form of God's guidance.

Some definitions

The inner voice of God the Holy Spirit is not audible to human ears, although God can speak and be heard audibly. The inner voice of God the Holy Spirit can only be heard in the realm of the thoughts of your mind and your spirit.

The inner witness occurs in the realm of Holy Spirit-given feelings in your human spirit. The inner voice does not refer to spiritual feelings, but to thoughts placed by God in your mind. These thoughts can come in words and/or resulting mental pictures.

The inner voice of His Spirit is referred to by God the Son in John 10:27 where He said,

My sheep listen to my voice.
Good News Version

This is what is referred to in 1 Kings 19:12 as the 'still small voice'. Isaiah 30:21 describes it this way:

If you wander off the road to the right or the left, you will hear his voice behind you saying, 'Here is the road. Follow it'.
Good News Version

If you are a true born-of-the-Spirit churchgoer, you will be the temple of the Holy Spirit. (See John 3:3–8, 1 Corinthians 6:19). Your human spirit unites with God's Spirit. If you are born of the Spirit, the Holy Spirit will guide you – through your spirit and your brain.

The attributes of man

Your spirit has thoughts, just as your physical body's brain has thoughts. When you die, your brain rots in the grave or turns to ashes, but your spirit keeps living forever. While your body lives, somehow the thoughts of your invisible spirit are linked to your physical brain.

When God speaks to you by the inner voice, He speaks to your spirit and your physical brain at the same time. It is His Holy Spirit speaking to you, living in your spirit.

This is not to say that your body is evil or that your spirit is trapped inside a supposedly evil body, as some foolish eastern religions teach. This is also not to suggest that a human is really two or three persons in one. A human is one whole, containing a spirit, a mind and a body. But it may help to understand these parts to consider them individually, just as a person can study a whole house by looking at each of its rooms separately.

Evidence that the human mind has a physical part and a non-material spiritual part is provided when a person has a stroke. A blood vessel in or near the physical brain forms a clot which cuts off the needed blood and oxygen supply to the brain. As a result, part of the brain dies. If the stroke kills some or most of the memory centres of the brain cells, the victim will find it hard to remember many or most of his experiences of past years. Some with strokes forget where they lived, how many children they have, much basic information about themselves and the world. Those who are senile, or have various brain diseases, often have similar lapses.

The non-material spirit lives on

If the physical brain was the only part of the human mind that God had given a Christian, then after suffering a stroke or becoming senile, everything a Christian had done in his life would be forgotten by him when he went to heaven, until his physical body was resurrected. Without his spirit being able to think and remember, all the lessons that God had taught him during his life would have been a waste of time. He would not be able to remember the events linked with these lessons, if such memories were recorded only in his physical brain.

Some Christians who have had a bad stoke or have gone senile, used to know the Scriptures backwards, but in many cases cannot now recall much of them, or remember their meaning. Unless it is true that the human mind is partly non-physical and a part of the human spirit, the ailing Christian would have learnt the Bible's teachings about God for nothing.

The truth is that your human mind is made up of a physical brain and a part which is in the non-material human spirit, both parts recording memories of all the events of your life. Any teachings of God's Scriptures that you learn in your life are also recorded in the non-physical memories of your spirit.

Your spirit has thoughts

The following is proof that the human spirit can think and remember things, just as the physical brain can. When a human dies, his spirit (if he is born again of the Holy Spirit Christian) goes to heaven. It is obvious to anyone attending his funeral that his physical body is buried in the ground.

After a number of years, his body disintegrates. His

physical brain is a part of his body which is buried in the ground. His spirit, when it goes to heaven, doesn't have its physical brain attached to it.

Therefore, does this mean that the spirit of a person whose body has died, is unable to think thoughts? Does this mean that his spirit doesn't have a mind? The answer to this must be 'No'.

For proof, turn to 1 Corinthians 2:11:

> **It is only a person's own spirit within him that knows all about him.**
> *Good News Version*

This verse clearly talks of a human spirit knowing and thinking.

It would be foolish for myself or anyone else to say whether or not a human spirit had a spiritual stomach, spiritual lungs, spiritual bowels, spiritual kidneys and so on. All such discussion would enter realms about which the Holy Scriptures do not give an answer and would be merely guessing or speculation. Such speculation about things which the Bible doesn't give specific details can lead to deception such as in occult-spiritualist groups. Beware of this!

Further proof that the human spirit can think things is found in Revelation 6:9–10. Here, the Apostle John speaks of the spirits of believers, who have died, speaking, thinking and remembering things from their lives on earth. If the human spirit was only a cloud, something like spiritual smoke, it could not do what John describes.

Do not take any of the above analysis to suggest that a human has two separate minds. For every human has only one mind. But for the purpose of study, it is important to dissect the human mind into its two parts, so that it becomes easier to understand ourselves and to understand how God speaks to us by His Holy Spirit.

A human is made up of feet, hands, stomach, eyes, ears and other parts. These are separate parts, but they all join to form one whole human. In the same way, the human mind is one, but with two parts. Trying to understand how this can be so is just as difficult as trying to understand how Jesus could be fully man and fully God at the same time. Limited human words cannot adequately explain either of these things. Many needless arguments about these things can ocur among Christians because of the limitations of words.

See also Matthew 26:41 and Luke 1:47 for further evidence that the human spirit can think things.

So just as in the last section on the inner witness, we saw that a human spirit has spiritual feelings, so too can a human spirit think things.

The two types of human spirits

When you are born again, your spirit and the Spirit of Jesus become one spirit (Romans 8:16). They become united as though they were married (Ephesians 5:31–32).

As a result of this uniting, the spirit of a born-again person becomes perfect and has within it all knowledge of what God's will is. God the Holy Spirit is dwelling in the human's spirit and 1 Corinthians 2:11 says that the Spirit of God knows everything about God. The Spirit of God talks to the spirit and physical brain of a human, from His dwelling-place in the human's spirit.

Someone who does not have the Spirit of God living within his human spirit will have his physical brain and emotions often guided by his human spirit to do things which flout His Will. 1 Corinthians 2:14 says:

> **Whoever does not have the Spirit cannot receive the gifts that come from God's Spirit. Such a person cannot understand them; they are nonsense to him, because their value can be judged on a spiritual basis.**
> *Good News Version*

An unbeliever is spiritually dead to the Spirit of Jesus. This person cannot really trust his human spirit to tell him what is good and what is bad.

But someone who has God the Holy Spirit united to his spirit by being born again, will have a human spirit eager to *always* obey Him.

The Apostle Paul said in Romans 7:22 that his inner being (his Holy Spirit-controlled human spirit) delighted to obey the law of God. Paul's spirit loved to obey the teachings of God's Holy Scripture. This willingness of a human spirit (united to the Holy Spirit) to obey God's will in everything was foretold by Ezekiel 36:26–27:

> **A new heart will I give you, and a new spirit will I put within you, and I will take away the stony heart out of your flesh and give you a heart of flesh. And I will put My Spirit within you and cause you to walk in My statutes and you shall heed My ordinances and do them.**
> *Amplified Version*

The same prophecy of what would occur in the lives of unbelievers who came to be born again of the Holy Spirit was stated in Ezekiel 11:19–20 and 2 Corinthians 5:17. Romans 8:10 expresses this also:

> **But if Christ lives in you, (then although your natural) body is dead by reason of sin and guilt, the spirit is alive because of the righteousness....**
> *Amplified Version*

A human who is a born-again Christian has the total desire in his human spirit to obey God's will.

The born-again human spirit has the potential in it to know everything about God's will. As 1 Corinthians 2:11 says, the Spirit of God understands everything about the will of God. Since a person who has been born again in his human spirit has the Spirit of Christ in him, the potential to know God's will is there.

Your human spirit is the vessel

We shouldn't look to our own human spirit to give us

guidance. This would be making a god of our human spirit. Instead, we should constantly look to God to give us guidance, remembering that the inner voice and the inner witness of God the Holy Spirit are firstly, spoken or spiritually felt in our human spirit. Then, this information is passed on to the physical brain. The human spirit is merely the vessel through which the Spirit of God guides.

The condition of our physical brains

Paul had a war inside himself, as most other Christians have (see Romans 7:15–25). His spirit wanted to always obey God (Romans 7:22). But his natural brain and physical emotions often wanted to disobey God's will, or did not want to even try to find his will. In Romans 7:23 Paul says:

> **But I see a different law at work in my body – a law that fights against the law which my mind approves of.**
> *Good News Version*

Where Paul talks here about his mind, he is talking about his spirit or the part of his physical brain that wanted to do God's will.

Your physical brain is like a computer, but it is very limited when compared to God's mind. Proof of these limitations are the following points. Our physical brain operates on one language (unless a person has learned a few languages). It can't totally understand how it is possible for the universe to never end; it finds it very hard to understand spiritual things.

Your physical emotions mostly tend towards selfish attitudes – jealousy, anger, envy, fear, resentment. But your spirit, because you have the Holy Spirit in you, takes on His perfect knowledge, perfect love, perfect feelings and perfect unselfishness.

Romans 7:15–25 clearly expresses what will happen to you. Your physical brain and its emotions will sometimes try to encourage you to disobey God's will. Wrong teachings and attitudes have been fed into your physical brain (which, like a computer, can be programmed) by relatives and friends, and by the sort of books, television shows, music and other influences that conflict with God's will as found in the Bible. This is what is meant by the influence of the world (The word 'world' in the Bible is not defined as the physical earth but as 'the non-Christian attitudes prevalent among many people in all nations').

Since once, all people were controlled by thoughts which came into their heads from demons, before they were born again Ephesians 2:2, 2 Timothy 2:26), their physical brains and their emotions tend to want to do bad things.

All people, who are born on Earth, are born spiritually dead, not filled with the Holy Spirit at birth (see Romans 5:12–15).

No humans until they are born again have the ability to love unselfishly the way that Jesus commanded us to do in Matthew 22:34–40. This is because in Matthew 22:34–40, Jesus commanded us to love God and to love people with agape love.

The word 'agape' was used in the original Greek New Testament to refer to love that comes from God alone. In the Greek, 1 John 4:8 says that God is 'agape'. Also, Galatians 5:22 uses the word 'agape' when talking about love as a fruit of the Holy Spirit. In these verses, the Greek words which refer to human love are not used. These words are 'phileo' and 'storge'.

Human love is not totally evil. However, it is tainted by selfishness and does not come up to God's standards as a result.

Agape is the only totally unselfish type of love. Loving with agape love is impossible for humans to do unless they have the Spirit of Jesus living in their human spirits.

The often quoted Chapter in the Bible on love in 1 Corinthians 13 is not talking about human phileo love. 1 Corinthians 13 is talking about God's agape love and what it can do.

Before people are born again, the absence of agape in

them tends to train the physical part of their minds and emotions towards selfishness.

Millions of decisions

Are you going to listen to the inner guidance of God the Holy Spirit speaking to your human spirit and physical brain? Or are you going to let your physical brain rebel against the obedient attitude that your born-again human spirit has? (See Romans 7:22.) Until the day you die, you will have to face millions of decisions of whether to obey God's Spirit speaking to your spirit and brain.

Confess your sin

If you do make a mistake and disobey, you must immediately confess your sin and God will forgive you (see 1 John 1:9). Every time in your life that you disobey God's will, as revealed by the Holy Scriptures and the inner guidance of the Spirit of Christ, you must clear its effect on your physical brain's memories and on your conscience.

Confession and bringing every thought of your physical brain into obedience to Christ (see 2 Corinthians 10:5) brings about this cleansing. Obedience to Christ means obedience to the teachings of His Holy Scriptures and to the guidance of His Holy Spirit.

Even though a weaker Christian often does not seek to hear the guidance of God's Spirit, He still tries to speak to him. The weaker Christian, when the Spirit of Jesus speaks to him in these ways, often rebels. He dismisses the guidance by imagining that his own mind must have thought to do this course of action. God's Spirit after this event will often still try to get the guidance through. The person's physical brain will feel torn as a result.

As a Christian, be careful not to allow your physical brain's reasonings, your physical emotions, the thoughts that demons put in your head each day and the things that other people want you to do, to encourage you to disobey the inner guidance of the Spirit of Christ (or disobey the teachings of Holy Scripture). 1 Thessalonians 5:19 says:

Do not quench (suppress or subdue) the (Holy) Spirit.
Amplified Version

Ephesians 4:30 means the same:

and do not grieve the Holy Spirit of God.
Amplified Version

Too many Christians are at present quenching and grieving the Spirit of God. As a result, they are causing extra troubles in their lives which God would like to help them avoid. Some Christians end up disobeying the guidance of the Holy Spirit so much that they backslide (see Timothy 1:19).

Even if people obey God's will day by day, they will still have troubles in their lives. 1 Peter 1:6–7 proves this. Trials are opportunities to prove God's care for us. But who wants to add the extra troubles that are needlessly caused by disobeying God?

Obedience brings victory

The situation of hundreds of Christians grieving and quenching the Holy Spirit by disobeying the inner guidance of God the Holy Spirit may be compared with worldly armies that have soldiers who disobey the orders of their generals. As a result, they are often defeated.

Christians should instead be like Roman armies. The Roman soldiers were mostly incredibly obedient to their generals. As a result they usually defeated larger, less disciplined, less obedient armies of Germanic tribes, Egyptians, Greeks, Britons and other nationalities. Small disciplined Roman armies for centuries defeated most armies that they came against.

How much more should Christians obey a God who is totally loving, totally unselfish, and knows everything about everything, when one considers that Roman soldiers obeyed often to the finest details the commands of their often selfish hard-hearted generals.

We should all look at ourselves as being soldiers who aim to be more obedient to the Spirit of Jesus and His Scriptures and to be more disciplined in our Christian lives (see 2 Timothy 2:3–4). This is a part of growing in holiness. But, just like the soldiers, we must train ourselves to be more obedient to His will (with the help and strength of God the Holy Spirit). This is a process that must continually occur until the day we die. We should not give up just because we may make some mistakes in the process of growing in holiness and obedience to God.

Let God rule your brain

After the resurrection of your physical body (see 1 Corinthians 15:12–58), the physical part of your mind and emotions will be reunited with your perfect spirit which will be in heaven. When the physical part of your mind is resurrected, it will be made totally holy. It will then no longer encourage you to get out of God's will.

But at the present time, your physical brain and its emotions must be, day by day, brought under the control of the teaching of the Word of God (see 2 Corinthians 10:5), and under the control of the Spirit of God (see Romans 8:5–8, Galatians 5:16). Otherwise, it will lead you to do bad things in your life. Galatians 5:16 says,

> **But I say, walk and live habitually in the Holy Spirit –
> responsive to and controlled by and guided by the Spirit,
> then you will certainly not gratify the cravings and
> desires of the flesh – of human nature without God.**
> *Amplified Version*

In this verse, the flesh is referring to any part of your physical body and brain not controlled by the person and will of God the Holy Spirit. The dictionary definition of the word 'flesh' as being 'the body' is not exactly the same as the original Bible definition of the word.

The inner voice of God's Spirit occurs thousands of times in the life of a strong Christian. Hearing God with a voice that can be heard with human ears may only happen once in a strong Christian's life, if at all. You shouldn't try to force God to speak to you in a way that can be heard with your human ears, because a demon may imitate Him. As 2 Corinthians 11:14 says:

> **Even Satan can disguise himself to look like an angel of light.**
> *Good News Version*

Let God speak to you in the way that He wants.

The inner voice and inner witness together

When you are waiting on God in prayer seeking to know His will, often this will occur: You will get an inner witness of the Holy Spirit at the same time that God speaks to you by the inner voice of His Holy Spirit.

The reason why God gives you both sometimes is:

1 if you just had a peace or a joy in your spirit, but this peace was not related to your physical brain having in it some particular course of action that God wanted you to do, you would be thinking, 'I know that I have an inner witness of peace and joy from God's Spirit, but I don't know what this spiritual sense of peace and joy is guiding me to do'.

For example, you are praying about which one of four jobs you should take. If you than have an inner witness of peace and joy in your spirit, but this inner witness occurs while your mind is blank and isn't thinking about or picturing any of these four jobs, you wouldn't clearly know which one of the four jobs you are having the inner witness about.

2 If you had just had a voice in your thoughts without an inner witness of peace and joy in your spirit from God's Spirit, you possibly wouldn't know whether the thought came from God or from a demon or from your own brain's human reasonings. The inner voice is only spoken in your thoughts. Unless you have the inner witness of peace and joy in your spirit at the same time, you possibly wouldn't know if it was from God or not.

On some occasions, though, God will give you only an inner witness in your spirit without Him also speaking to you by the inner voice in your thoughts. This occurs in the following way.

When waiting on God in prayer seeking to know His Will, you can often have His Spirit give you an inner witness, by allowing your brain to first picture each of the alternatives that you can think God may want you to do. While you are, with eyes closed, picturing each alternative, praise and thank God for many many minutes and tell God in truth that you will do whatever He desires.

While picturing each of these alternatives, if one of them is God's will, God may on your first day of waiting on Him in prayer or on some future day, give you the inner witness of peace and joy to tell you that this is God's will for your life.

This is all very Scriptural. God in Acts 13:2 reveals that the Holy Spirit speaks to us when we are praising, worshipping and thanking God. Also, Romans 12:1–2 reveals that if we commit our whole selves over to God's control, willing to do whatever He says, He will then reveals His perfect will to us. Study these Scriptures!

Guidance about intercession

Here is an example of God speaking by the inner voice. It is also an example of how God sometimes uses other believers to give us confirmation that what we think is Him speaking to us by an inner voice and/or inner witness of his Holy Spirit, is in fact really from Him.

Between 1976 and Autumn 1977, I read about the life of 'Father' Nash, who was a retired Presbyterian minister. He used to intercede for hours for the evangelistic campaigns of the dedicated evangelist Charles Finney. While reading about Nash, I used to have a sense of great peace and joy in myself when I thought about or pictured myself interceding for hours also. This sense of great peace and joy would happen whenever at other times while praying, I would think of myself interceding. I mostly had this sense of peace while I was praying. However, since I was immature in the things of God, I wasn't sure if it was an inner witness of His Holy Spirit.

I also seemed to have thoughts come into my mind at other times about Him wanting me to intercede.

Because God knew that I wasn't sure if these thoughts about me being an intercessor were inner voices of His Spirit and whether these feelings of peace were inner witnesses in my spirit, He spoke to two other people about this matter. For when I went to a prayer meeting of a group of people from a church in Penrith, this happened.

One man after praying, praising God, thanking Him and listening to Him, said to me that God wanted me to be an intercessor for other people. (Intercessors are people who pray mostly by themselves or with a group, for other individuals, groups or nations). This man didn't know anything about me. I had only said, 'Hello', to him on this day for the first time. I said nothing else to him.

Then a woman who knew a little about me said to me that God had given her the same message. This woman didn't know that God had been speaking to me about intercession also.

So God used these two Christians to confirm what I thought was Him speaking to me, really was Him and wasn't my own imagination or a demon.

We need to grow spiritually

Usually, God only gives other Christians a Word of the

Lord or a revelation to pass on to you if He sees that you need confirmation, that what you already think you have in your spirit in the form of an inner witness and what you already have in your mind in the form of an inner voice of His Spirit, is really Him speaking. This is because God mainly wants to lead you himself by His Holy Spirit. This is seen in Romans 8:14, 8:5–8, 9:1, Galatians 5:16–18 and 5:25.

God doesn't want you to be too reliant on what He has revealed to other people. Being too reliant on other people would make a personal relationship to Him unnecessary and could lead you to be easily tricked by false prophets and false teachers.

If I had been able to clearly see His guidance myself, Jesus would not have needed to have told the above man and woman to pass this message on to me. This is why we all need to keep growing more mature spiritually and not stay as spiritual babes who don't know what their Father is trying to say to them.

Years later this guidance about intercession has come to pass. From 1980 onwards, I have felt a constant desire in my mind and spirit to pray about the spiritual state of Australia and about many other things.

Evan Roberts

Another example of the inner voice is seen in the life of Evan Roberts. Roberts was one of the evangelists that God used in 1905–6 to lead thousands of unbelievers to Himself in the Welsh Revival.

In this spiritual renewal of Christianity, 10% of the whole population of Wales was converted. Many Welsh churchgoers grew in holiness and devotion to God at this time also.

Evan Roberts was a young coalminer whom God led to be one of His evangelists. As Roberts was praying one day and listening to Jesus, he received guidance. God's Spirit kept speaking into Roberts' mind the suggestion that

Roberts would one day effectively preach in the school-room of his village to his old friends and to the young people of the village.

As he heard these suggestions in his thoughts, these God-given suggestions created mental pictures of this occuring. He could picture all of these people sitting in rows while he preached to them.

Roberts was at first afraid that these thoughts were from Satan. These suggestions kept coming back to Roberts' mind over the following months when he would pray about God's will.

These suggestions need to be tested to see if they are really from God. Firstly, they passed the test of being in agreement with the Holy Scriptures. For in the Holy Scriptures, Jesus commanded Christians to preach the Word of God (Matthew 28:19–20, Mark 16:15) and God through the mouth of Paul said that some Christians are called by Him to be evangelists (see Ephesians 4:11–12). Also, Evan was not being told to hate anyone, steal from anyone, commit adultery, be a homosexual, take drugs or do any other things which were contrary to the teachings of Scripture.

These suggestions in Roberts' mind also passed the second major test of seeing if they were from God: Roberts didn't have a sense of uneasiness or lack of peace in his spirit as he prayed on a number of occasions about this seeming inner voice from God.

He needed the inner witness, because even though the Holy Scripture says that it is godly to preach, not all men are called to preach.

Roberts then concluded that this inner voice was not from Satan, but was from God. He then began to take steps so that he could obey this Word of the Lord spoken through the inner voice and the inner witness.

The pastor of the local village church told Roberts that preaching to these villagers would be hard and results would be little. Roberts refused to listen to such thoughts. Instead, he concentrated on believing that the Word of the

Lord that God the Holy Spirit had spoken to him would come to pass.

Roberts had a right to exercise this type of faith and certainty because Romans 10:17 says that faith comes from hearing the Word of the Lord.

Not long after, Jesus by the power of the Spirit, brought into circumstances the fulfilment of the above guidance. For Roberts preached in exactly the way that the inner voice told him.

As a result of this Word from the Holy Spirit, Roberts' faith in and obedience to this inner voice from Him, the Holy Spirit was able to use Roberts in this village to convert to Jesus, hundreds of previously ungodly hard hearted miners and tinplate workers. The churches in the village were filled with eager people at all hours wanting to constantly pray, sing and testify about what Jesus was doing in their lives. What a tremendous result!

Chapter 7   Inner voice of the Holy Spirit

1 What is the inner voice of the Holy Spirit?
2 Can the human spirit think?
3 Why does God sometimes speak to believers by an inner voice and inner witness at the same time?

8

Circumstances

Signs in one's circumstances sometimes reveal God's will. But circumstances don't always reveal His will. Many churchgoers need to learn these two things.

Some people are superstitious about circumstances. Every time someone knocks on the door they believe that God has sent the door-knocker. This sort of Christian should realise that it could be God's will the person is at the door. But then again, the person knocking at the door may be disobeying His perfect will by coming, for example, to give a false revelation.

If the Christian has a superstitious attitude that all circumstances reveal God's perfect will, then this may happen: The door-knocker giving a false revelation may result in the Christian disobeying God through the Christian believing and acting on false revelation.

Some circumstances reveal God's will. Others don't.

King David

If King David had looked to his circumstances as his only or main sign of God's will when Saul's soldiers were hunting him, he would never have believed the Word of the Lord, spoken by the Holy Spirit to him, that he was going to be king (see 1 Chronicles 11:2).

In fact, nearly every circumstance suggested that he

would be killed by the army of Israel (see 1 Samuel, chapters 19–31). He also ran the risk of being handed over by some Israelite such as Nabal to Saul for execution (see 1 Samuel 25). However, God's will for David was the opposite of what these circumstances suggested. God didn't want David to die, but wanted him to become King of Israel.

Don't be misled by signs

Just because God allows something to happen, this doesn't mean that this event is His perfect will. For example, God doesn't want people to murder. However, He allows them to do it.

Because God doesn't want to take away our precious gift of free-will, He has to put up with humans often using this free-will to decide to do things which are not His perfect will.

We must ignore circumstances that suggest that God's will for us is something which opposes Bible principles and the inner witness and the inner voice of His Holy Spirit. These sorts of circumstances are not to be taken as guidance.

Only some of our circumstances reveal what God wants us to do. For example, a temptation to get drunk comes before a Christian who used to be an alcoholic. He can't in this case say that God is 'opening doors' and bringing circumstances about which show that He wants him to get drunk. Circumstances here contradict God's Word in Ephesians 5:18 which says,

Do not get drunk with wine.
Good News Version

Likewise, just because a Christian friend or leader tells you to become a missionary, doesn't mean necessarily that God is bringing about circumstances to lead you to be a missionary. God may be influencing the Christian friend or leader to say this to you, but then again maybe He is not. You need to wait on God in prayer until His Holy Spirit reveals to your mind or spirit whether these circumstances reveal His will for you.

A similar circumstance which would need a lot of prayer would be if you were offered 13 good jobs on the same day. In this situation, you couldn't say that God was 'opening the door of circumstances' for you to have all 13 jobs.

Some people foolishly pray, 'Lord, if you want me to marry John, will you 'open the door' of circumstances so that he will ask me to marry him'. Just because John is later allowed by God to ask you to marry him, this doesn't mean that God wants you to marry him. The inner witness and the inner voice of the Holy Spirit are far better guides to God's will.

Be just as careful of circumstances as you are of inner witnesses, dreams and so on, when seeking God's will! Wait on God in prayer until you are sure that they are a sign from Him which reveals His will to you.

How do you think David, Joshua, Elijah, Elisha, Paul, Peter and other strong believers knew so many times what the Holy Spirit wanted them to do? Firstly, they studied God's Word. Secondly, they constantly day-by-day waited on God in prayer, trusting Him to reveal His will to them through the inner guidance of the Holy Spirit – and, on rarer occasions, through circumstances, dreams and so on.

Scriptural examples of signs

Circumstances can on some occasions reveal God's will. Jesus, dying on the Cross and performing miracles for people because He loved the human race, are circumstances which reveal some things about God's will.

Also, remember Jesus said in Matthew 16:2–3:

When the sun is setting, you say, 'We are going to have fine weather, because the sky is red', and early in the

morning you say, 'It is going to rain because the sky is red and dark'. You can predict the weather by looking at the sky, but you cannot interpret the signs concerning these times.
Good News Version

This verse clearly shows that sometimes circumstances are a sign of what God's perfect will is.

But we should note that the signs of the times (i.e. circumstances at the time of Jesus) could only be understood as revealing God's will through a knowledge of the Old Testament. Anyone who didn't have a revelation of the prophecies of the Old Testament could never have been able to interpret what the circumstances (i.e. signs of the times) meant.

For only people who knew Isaiah 53:1 – 12, Daniel 9: 24 – 26, Genesis 49:10, Deuteronomy 18:18 – 19, Psalm 22, Micah 5:2, Zechariah 9:9 – 10 and Malachi 3:1, could have the knowledge from God to understand what the coming of John the Baptist and the events of Jesus' life meant. The circumstances were only signs to those who had a Holy Spirit revelation of the Scriptures above.

In the Scriptures, there are a number of other examples of believers being given signs of God's will in their circumstances. Jeremiah 32:6–8 is the first example. These verses show clearly though that Jeremiah didn't take signs in circumstances as being his only guide of God's will. In verse 8, we see that Jeremiah also took the inner guidance of God the Holy Spirit as being his other indicator of God's will in this situation.

1 Samuel 10:1–9 is the second example. These verses relate signs in circumstances as sometimes being a confirmation of inner guidance of the Holy Spirit. Verses 7 and 9 mention the word 'signs', as do Isaiah 7:10–14 and Isaiah 20:1–6. In Isaiah 20:1–6, without inner guidance from God the Holy Spirit, it would be impossible to relate circumstances of a prophet running around naked as being a sign of what was going to happen to Egypt and Sudan. A

prophet running around naked could be taken as a sign that he was mad or a sign of thousands of other things, if God's Spirit had not given a revelation of what this circumstance meant.

Isaiah 37:30–32 is another example of God giving a sign of His will in circumstances. However, the circumstance of only having wild grain to eat that year and the circumstance of having grain and grapes the following year could not be taken as a sign of anything without the inner guidance of God's Spirit which Isaiah is seen to have received in Isaiah 37:21–22. In Isaiah 38:1–8, without the guidance of the Holy Spirit, the circumstance of the sun dial going backwards could have meant anything.

A major problem

One of the major problems for people who look too much to circumstances to reveal God's will is the fact that they have a tendency to regard problems, troubles and suffering in their lives as showing that they are not in His will.

For example, God's Spirit by an inner witness of peace and joy in his human spirit may lead a person, like the above, to work at a particular firm. However, if he is persecuted there because he is a Christian and if he finds the work very hard, this sort of person will probably take these circumstances as meaning that God doesn't want him to work there. If he looks to circumstances as signs, he will probably quit and disobey God.

Just because in our circumstances, we are having troubles, trials and suffering, this doesn't mean that we are out of God's will. For many times, God leads us to do things which are easy and involve no trouble. However, sometimes His Spirit will guide us to do something which will cause trouble and suffering for us.

This is seen in the following examples from Holy Scripture. Firstly, the Israelites were led into the desert between Egypt and the Promised Land of Canaan. In this desert, the Israelites were faced with the terrible problem of finding fresh water. Remember that people can only live three days without water (see Exodus 15:22 – 27 and 17: 1 – 7). The Israelites also had to find food in a dry, barren desert (see Exodus 16:1–36), and faced the threat of death from demon worshipping Amalekites (see Exodus 17: 8 – 16).

Secondly, Joshua was led by God the Holy Spirit to fight against armies that were stronger than his own army. This involved the danger of suffering and death. (See Numbers 13:27–29 and 13:32–33 and Joshua Chapters 1 to 11.)

Thirdly, David was led into a situation where King Saul's soldiers were trying to kill him. Constantly, each day, David had the threat of being caught and killed (see 1 Samuel Chapters 19 to 27 and 31).

Fourthly, the prophet Jonah was led by God the Holy Spirit to go to preach to the wicked Assyrian people (see Jonah 1:1–3 and Chapters 3 and 4). The Assyrians used to slowly cut off the hands, feet, nose, ears and other parts of an opposing captured soldier until the person died in agony, or they would skin him alive. Even though Jonah was not a soldier, he risked similar treatment if he went there.

The Apostle Paul was in God's perfect will when he suffered so many things. Acts 9:15–16 and Acts 21:10–11 reveal that circumstances of trouble don't always mean that we are out of His will. Acts 9:15–16 (when talking about what God said to Ananias about Paul) says:

> **The Lord said to him, 'Go because I have chosen him to serve me, to make my name known to the Gentiles and kings and to the people of Israel. And I Myself will show him all that he must suffer for my sake'.**
> *Good News Version*

But remember God will only lead you to do something which results in trouble, trials and suffering, if He sees that you will grow stronger spiritually and emotionally as a result. God wants to see you grow up. Many adults are really only children in adults' bodies. God wants such people to grow and mature spiritually and emotionally.

Here is an example of what God's Spirit may lead you to do: He may lead you to work at a place where you have trouble and suffering, so that you will lose the sinful human tendency of doing things just to have other people like you and not criticise you.

Israel wanted a king

Circumstances alone cannot be taken as a reliable guide of God's perfect will, as the Scriptures prove. For example, God told Samuel (see 1 Samuel Chapter 8) that it was not his perfect will for the nation of Israel to have a king. God, however, against His perfect will, allowed Israel to have a king. 1 Samuel 8:4–7 says,

> **Then all the leaders of Israel met together, went to Samuel in Ramah and said to him, 'Look, you are getting old and your sons don't follow your example. So then appoint a king to rule over us so that we will have a king, as other countries have'. Samuel was displeased with their request for a king, so he prayed to the Lord and the Lord said, 'Listen to everything the people say to you. You are not the one they have rejected. I am the one they have rejected as their king'.**
> *Good News Version*

These Scriptures indicate that God's perfect will was for the Israelites not to have a king. God knew it was best if He was their only king.

If the people living in the time of Saul had gone mainly by circumstances in deciding what was God's will (as many churchgoers do today through ignorance of the Scriptures and of the inner guidance from God through inner witnesses and inner still small voices), they would have said, 'It must be God's perfect will for us to have a king. This is because He has allowed the circumstances to occur where we have a king. He is controller of the universe, so whatever happens in circumstances must be His perfect will'.

The people who would say this would have failed to have drawn a distinction between what God causes and what He permits or allows. There is a big difference between these two things. For example, in the Book of Job, God allowed Satan to attack Job, but He didn't cause or force Satan to do this. (Job 1:6–22, especially verse 12, and Job 2:1–10, especially verse 6.)

Many people in the time of Saul probably prayed for a king, in a similar manner to many people today. Since they did not know a lot about getting guidance from God, they therefore prayed that He would 'open the door of circumstance' if it was His will for them to have what they were asking for.

Samuel knew that it wasn't God's perfect will that they have a king. We see in 1 Samuel 8:4–9 that Samuel didn't take circumstances as being his main guide of what God's will was. Instead, Samuel went by the inner guidance of God the Holy Spirit.

Probably, many Israelites would have said, 'Silly Samuel! He says that it is not God's will for us to have a king. He says that God has spoken into his mind by an inner voice that it is not God's perfect will. Samuel is supposed to be a prophet, but he doesn't even know how to find God's will. Look at circumstances! God has given us a king. He has answered our 'if it by thy will' prayer by opening the door of circumstances. Poor Samuel! Doesn't he know that everything that happens in life is God's perfect will?'

The above Israelites have a foolish understanding of what is called the 'Sovereignty of God'. The Sovereignty of God in its correct Bible-based form refers to the fact that God is the total controller and ruler of the universe and that no event can occur without Him either causing or allowing it. No human or demon can do anything unless God permits him or her to do it. (See Job 1:6–12.)

Some religious people who have a false understanding of the Sovereignty of God teach that every event that occurs on Earth is God's perfect will. They teach that He has caused them all to occur. They forget that God in His own sovereign will has decided to limit His own power in many circumstances, so that humans and demons can have a free-will with which they can decide what to do.

Fate or destiny

These people, with a false understanding of the Sovereignty of God, have attitudes more similar to the attitudes of many ancient pagan Greeks. These ancient Greeks suggested that every event that occurred was the will of the so-called 'gods'. This attitude is called fate or destiny.

God in Isaiah 65:11–12, condemns fate and destiny ideas. In these verses, God is seen to have told Isaiah to speak against the fate and destiny teachings associated with the two Babylonian gods called Meni and Gad. The pagan Babylonians taught fate and destiny ideas. Many of the present day Muslims have silly fate or destiny ideas also.

The Bible's teaching

The Scriptures teach that life on Earth is a mixture of:

1 Circumstances that God causes, e.g.
   a) God didn't just allow the universe to be created. He caused it to be created (Hebrews 1:2–3)
   b) God caused the human race to be created (see Genesis 2:7),
   c) God will cause Satan to be bound (see Revelation 20:1–2).

2 Circumstances that God allows, e.g.
   a) Satan attacked people (Job 2:7 and Mark 9:17–27) and interfered with nature, in storms and lightning only because God allowed him to (Job 1:12 and 1:16–19)
   b) God only allows but doesn't cause people to murder,

rape or hate or decide not to obey His will in other ways.

We can't obey God's will without the help of the Holy Spirit, but we can either accept or reject the help of God the Holy Spirit enabling us to obey His will.

Free-will

People and demons only have a certain amount of free-will because God in His sovereign will allows it. No one is powerful enough to have free-will unless God gives it to him. But once He has given free-will, humans or demons are then responsible for their own decisions.

God, only in rare circumstances, forces people to do things which are against the free-will gift that He has caused or forced them to have in the first place. In Exodus 9:12, it says that God forced the heart of Pharoah to be stubborn towards what Moses said to him. Refer also to Romans 9:10–13 and Romans 11:8 for similar examples.

However, most decisions that humans make are not caused or forced upon them by God.

That is why it is foolish to believe that just because a person offers you a job or someone wants to marry you, that this must be God opening the door of circumstances to show you His will. These circumstances will only be signs of God's will if the person who offers you the job or if the peson who asks you to marry or if the person who asks you to lead the church prayer meeting is doing what he is doing in obedience to an inner voice or inner witness of God the Holy Spirit.

Sometimes, unbelievers are told by God in their thoughts to do something. Mostly, however, unbelievers don't recognize this as God speaking to them. Sometimes, they unknowingly obey this inner voice. At other times, they don't.

Take an example from the Scriptures: Nebuchadnezzar, King of Babylon, was first of all a pagan, as shown by his setting up of a gold statue for everyone to worship. He made a law that anyone who didn't worship this pagan idol would be killed. Daniel 3:1–7 reveals all this. But note that at a time before this, in Daniel Chapter 2, God spoke to Nebuchadnezzar in a dream.

Just because an unbeliever unknowingly obeys God a few times, this doesn't get the unbeliever to Heaven. For a person needs a continual personal love-faith-born of the Holy Spirit relationship to God to get to heaven.

Unfavourable circumstances

Unfavourable circumstances do not always reveal that you are out of God's will. They only do on some occasions. For as has been shown before, sometimes you can have unfavourable troubled circumstances while being right in God's perfect will.

Only the inner guidance of God the Holy Spirit can reveal if the unfavourable circumstances are a result of you being out of God's perfect will or not. Remember that the inner guidance of the Holy Spirit and the Holy Scriptures are far more reliable revealers of God's will for your life than circumstances. Don't be superstitious about circumstances like Muslims and like many ancient pagans!

Circumstances in the long run always come into agreement with what God has shown you by an inner witness or an inner voice or a dream or so on. However, very often in the short term, they will be the opposite of what God reveals to you by His Holy Spirit.

For example, God told Abraham in a vision that he was going to have a son. (See Genesis 15:1–5.) However, for 25 years after this, circumstances were the opposite of this guidance. No son was born to Abraham for all these years.

However, at the end of 25 years, circumstances changed to agree with the revelation that God gave Abraham 25 years before. If Abraham, over the 25 years, had looked at his circumstances (his own and Sarah's physical inability to have a child), as his only or main guide of God's perfect will, he would have doubted the Words of the Lord which told him that he would be going to have a son. Study Romans 4:17–22.

Abraham didn't use circumstances as his main form of guidance. Instead, he exercised trust in the inner voices, dreams and visions that God gave him in Genesis 15:1–5, 17:1–22 and 18:1–15.

Conclusion

Therefore, circumstances are not a reliable guide of God's will. They must be confirmed by,

1 The words and teachings of Holy Scriptures and/or
2 The inner guidance in your thoughts and human spirit from God the Holy Spirit, before you can accept them as revealing God's will.

Don't try to work out God's will by praying 'open the door if it by thy will' prayers or by looking at circumstances alone.

Chapter 8   Circumstances

1 Can *all* circumstances be taken as signs of God's will?
2 Does God cause every event that happens on Earth or are millions of things only allowed by Him to occur?
3 Does being in unfavourable circumstances show that you are out of God's will?
4 What should be your attitude to circumstances in determining what God is trying to say to you?

9

Test all things
(1 Thessalonians 5:21)

Every day, we have in our minds, thoughts from our own human reasoning. Also each day, we have thoughts whispered into our minds by demons. So it is necessary for every Christian to know the difference between these and the inner voice of God the Holy Spirit.

We don't want to be deceived by cunning demonic spirits. Nor do we want to allow our lives to be dominated by our own human plans and aims, because so many times these are not God's will. As God says in Isaiah 55:9:

For as the heavens are higher than the earth, so are My ways higher than your ways, and My thoughts than your thoughts.
Amplified Version

There are two main ways of testing all 'guidance'.

The first test

The first way you can tell whether an inner voice is from God's Spirit or from your own mind or from demonic spirits is to check with the Bible. The Holy Scriptures will show if the voice is telling you to do or believe something opposite to or different from what God teaches.

For example, if the 'inner voice' tells you to try to communicate with spirits of the dead, you will know that this voice is a demon talking or is merely your own human reasoning. Deuteronomy 18:11 says not to try to talk to the spirits of the dead. *The Word and God the Holy Spirit never disagree.*

The second test

The second way that you can tell if the voice that you hear in your thoughts is the voice of God the Holy Spirit (who is living in your human spirit if you are really walking in a personal relationship to God) is this: You will have a tremendous sense of peace or joy or both in your spirit at the time that these thoughts come into your head. The inner voice and the inner witness often come together.

For example, you are waiting on God in prayer and you have the thought come into your mind that God wants you to go to visit your mother-in-law today to give her spiritual help. At the same time, you have a tremendous sense of peace or joy in your spirit. So this thought is God telling you by the inner voice to do this.

Here is a second example. While praying, you have a voice speak into your thoughts which tells you that God wants you to believe with certainty that your wife will miraculously have a baby. The voice in your thoughts says this, even though your wife is physically incapable of bearing a child. If you have tremendous peace in your spirit at the same time as you hear these thoughts, then this is God speaking to you. Remember that God spoke like this to Abraham.

This peace and joy will be in your spirit. It will not be in your human emotions or physical feelings. It may take you much practise and prayer to know the difference. But keep trying to learn the difference, even if you make a few mistakes. You must crawl before walking.

The peace and the joy of the inner witness will more readily accompany the inner voice of God the Holy Spirit if you follow the practises in the chapter 'Improving Your Ability to Recognize God's Voice'.

65

Sometimes, the inner voice will not be accompanied by the inner witness of peace or joy, but this is rarer. If this happens to you, you should wait on God to see if this seeming 'revelation' really is from Him. This is because it is harder to tell if an inner voice without the inner witness is from God or demons or your own mind.

An example

Here is one example of testing a revelation by the second way. I know someone who heard an evangelist in Australia say that the Holy Spirit had told him that India would become Communist in June 1980. This person had an inner witness of a very tight unpleasant feeling in his spirit (but not in his human emotions) when this evangelist said this. This inner witness was God saying that what the evangelist claimed was from Him, was not from Him at all.

Note though that if you have bad feelings in your human emotions, when hearing a true prophecy of God (e.g. if you heard Elijah predict famine), this is not an inner witness, but your own flesh.

Just as the inner witness of the Holy Spirit revealed, the evangelist was speaking his own thoughts and not God's thoughts. For India didn't become Communist by June 1980.

Note, however, that just because a Christian makes a mistake in getting guidance from God and says that something is from Him and we find out that it wasn't from Him, this doesn't necessarily mean that this person is a false prophet.

The person could possibly be a Christian who desires to obey God, but just made a mistake. We all can make mistakes in getting guidance from God, especially when we are spiritually immature. In Acts 20:30 though, Paul said that false prophets would be actual members of some local Christian churches.

More important points

Some churchgoers such as some (but not all) of the Quakers over-emphasise the importance of inner guidance. They don't check their so-called 'inner guidance from the Holy Spirit' against the teachings of the Scriptures. As a result, some of them say that God the Holy Spirit told them that people are not born with a sinful human nature and that homosexuality is not wrong.

In this case, so-called 'Holy Spirit inner guidance' is not from God the Holy Spirit at all. 1 Corinthians 6:9 and Romans 1:26–27 in the New Testament and Leviticus 18:22, Leviticus 20:13, Deuteronomy 23:17–18, 1 Kings 14:24 and 2 Kings 23:7 in the Old Testament all state that God says homosexuality is wicked. God the Holy Spirit wouldn't say one thing in the Holy Scriptures and then a different thing through inner guidance to some Quakers and to other churchgoers.

Also, note that Galatians 5:17–21, Romans 3:9–18 and 3:23 show that human nature is not good. God the Holy Spirit wouldn't give inner guidance to some churchgoers saying the opposite. God is not so ridiculous.

Some churchgoers down through church history, have accepted so-called 'inner guidance' that is contrary to the teachings of Holy Scriptures. As a result, many church teachers have rejected inner witnesses and inner voices of God the Holy Spirit altogether. These silly churchgoers have helped to bring into disrepute two Scripture-based forms of guidance from God.

All Christians should be willing to have all of their so-called revelations of the Holy Spirit tested and judged by a pastoral local church leadership that is very Scripture-based and centred on Jesus. This is especially so if the revelation is said by the person to be a Word of the Lord spoken by God the Holy Spirit to the Church as a whole or to another individual believer. 1 Thessalonians 5:19–21 says,

Do not quench (suppress or subdue) the (Holy) Spirit. Do not spurn the gifts and utterances of the prophets – do not depreciate prophetic revelations, nor despise inspired instruction or exhortation or warning. But test and prove all things (until you can recognize) what is good; (to that) hold fast.
Amplified Version

These verses show that we are not to reject revelations spoken directly by the Spirit of Jesus to us and indirectly through other Christians. They also show that we must test all of the things that are said to be revelations from God to see if they are really from Him.

Two checks

In summary, you can see if a revelation is really from God

a) by checking to see if the revelation is different from Bible principles (see 2 Timothy 3:16–17, Acts 17:11, 1 Corinthians 14:37–38 and Mark 7:1–13), and

b) by checking to see if you have the inner witness of peace and joy from the Holy Spirit (or a restlessness or lack of peace from the Holy Spirit) while thinking and/or praying about this thing which is said to be from Him (see Galatians 5:22, Romans 8:16, Colossians 3:15).

1 Corinthians 14:29 is another scripture which confirms that we must test and check anything which is said to be a revelation of God the Holy Spirit to the Church. This verse says:

So, let two or three prophets speak – those inspired to preach or teach – while the rest pay attention and weigh and discern what is said.
Amplified Version

68

Chapter 9 Test all things

1 What are the two main ways that you should test to see if what you think is God speaking to you, is really Him?
2 Why do you need to test all 'guidance' or 'voices' or 'revelations'?
3 In your Bible study group, share events which have occurred where you thought that God was speaking to you. Then have everyone or the leader test the 'guidance' by the two abovementioned ways.

10

The God-given mind...
What is it for?

Some preachers say that God had given us a mind and
common sense which He expects us to use in deciding
what we should do in our lives. They say that since our
minds and common sense are gifts of God, we should use
them to decide which job we should have, which town to
live in, which local congregation to go to, how much
furniture we should have, which car we should buy and
other similar questions.

These preachers have little knowledge of God's Holy
Scripture. They would lead us into disobedience to God
the Holy Spirit. This is because even though they are
correct in saying that a mind and common sense are
God-given gifts, they ignore the fact that these gifts only
operate properly when they are controlled by God the
Holy Spirit. Romans 8:6-7 in the Amplified Version
clearly shows this:

> **Now the mind of the flesh (which is sense and reason
> without the Holy Spirit) is death – death that comprises
> all the miseries arising from sin, both here and hereafter.
> But the mind of the Holy Spirit is both life and soul
> peace, both now and forever. That is because the mind of
> the flesh – with its carnal thoughts and purposes – is
> hostile to God; for it does not submit itself to God's Law,
> indeed it cannot.**

Verse 6 shows that God says the human mind, including its common sense and reason, that is not controlled by the presence and guidance of God's Spirit, is dead and useless. The verse does not say that human reason and common sense are evil. Instead, it is putting human reason and common sense in their right place.

Some churchgoers are taught to have spiritually dead minds by being taught to make their own decisions with their minds or reason and common sense alone. How tragic!

Reason and common sense

Reason can be defined as the ability of the human mind to mathematically calculate, deduce, find relationships between things, mentally picture and so on.

Common sense can be defined as knowledge gained through the experiences of your five physical senses and through other people telling you of the knowledge that they have gained via the experiences of their senses. The five physical senses are sight, hearing, smell, touch and taste.

The physical senses and our reasoning abilities are gifts of God. They are given in differing qualities to each person. They mostly work together in the process of human learning or deciding what to do. For example, a child learning from its father will use its seeing, hearing and reasoning abilities to absorb what the father is saying.

There is nothing evil about you learning to hammer a nail, cook a meal, clean your teeth or swim in a lake, by using your reason and five physical senses.

However, as a Christian, you must always keep your reasoning ability and common sense submitted to the control of God the Holy Spirit.

In practise, this means being always willing to totally ignore what your mind's reasoning ability and common sense tell you, even if:

a) the Scriptures teach something which your reasoning ability and common sense can't understand. For example, don't let the limitations of your human reason and common sense lead you to reject the truth that God exists in three persons – Father, Son and Holy Spirit, just because they can't understand how this could be true (see 2 Cor 3:17, Isaiah 9:6, John 5:17–18, 23–26, John 8:58).

b) the Spirit of Jesus gives you guidance to do something which to human reasoning and common sense seems foolish. For example, God's Spirit may reveal to you that He wants you, for a special purpose, to be able to run faster than horses (as Elijah did: see 1 Kings 18:45–46). Your reason and the experiences of your physical senses will most likely tell you that this is impossible. If you trust in them, you will end up doubting and disobeying God's will.

The same would apply if the Holy Spirit told you that He wanted you to walk on the water for some special purpose. Would you allow your reason and the experiences of your life and the reasonings and experiences of your friends and relatives, to cause you to doubt that God would empower you to do this, as Peter had done before he doubted?

Commit your reason to God

If you don't subordinate your mind's reasoning ability and common sense to the control of the Holy Spirit each day, you will not be a Spirit-controlled Christian. You will be a self-reliant weak Christian, because you will be ruled more by your reason and common sense than you are by God.

You must commit your reason and common sense to God's control the way that Romans 12:1–2, Galatians 5:16 and many other Bible verses command.

The physical senses have been given by God for a good

purpose. However, many humans make a 'god' of the experiences of their physical senses. They do this by accepting what their physical senses tell them, even in cases where the Scriptures or the guidance of the Holy Spirit says otherwise.

They forget that the physical senses were limited by God. God did this so that humans would not allow their physical senses to rule them instead of Him.

Limitations of physical senses

If you need proof of the limitations of the senses, here are a few examples.

- The human ear can't hear sounds that dogs can hear.
- When looking down a railway line, the human eyes wrongly suggest that the railway tracks meet.
- Human noses cannot smell certain things that some animals' noses can smell.
- To one person's tastebuds, a food may taste bitter. To another, it may taste sweet. Which tastebuds are giving the correct information?

There are many other examples which show the limitations of the physical senses and their variability in observing events.

The human reason has similar limitations as has been said in Chapter 7.

Common sense is limited to your experiences and the experiences that other people share with you. God has knowledge and experience of countless things that you and your parents, friends, teachers and others have never had. Hebrew 4:13 says:

> **And not a creature exists that is concealed from His sight but all things are opened and exposed, naked and defenseless to the eyes of Him with Whom we have to do.**
> *Amplified Version*

Refer also to 1 Samuel 16:7, Job 34:21, Job chapters 38 to 41 and Isaiah 55:8—9.

Therefore, if you limit your decision-making to other people's knowledge and experiences, you are limiting yourself greatly. Examples of humans limiting themselves in this way are seen in Chapter 12 'Results of Minds Not God-Controlled'.

In Chapter 13 'Examples of Incredible Trust in God's Guidance' and in the beginning of Chapter 18 'Extra Points To Note', good examples are given of people not limiting themselves in the above way. God will probably test you also to see if you will obey Him when He guides you to do something which your human reason and common sense cannot understand or have not experienced.

Subjectivity of those who reject inner guidance

Many churchgoers reject the notion of being guided inwardly by the Holy Spirit and by signs in our circumstances. They say that making decisions in this way is too subjective. Subjectivity is where you decide what is true by your own thoughts, feelings and impressions without testing them by some external standard of truth.

The people who argue this way sound as though they are so stable and spiritually mature. They say that they make their decisions on the basis of what the Scriptures say and on the basis of sound judgement.

They say that the Scriptures give good general principles about deciding whom to marry, where to live and so on. This is true. But because the Scriptures do not specifically tell you whom to marry, where to live, which job to have and so on, the above 'stable, mature' churchgoers end up in practise using their reason and common sense to make the final decision.

For example, the Scriptures teach not to have a job which involves stealing, murdering, immorality, lying or occult. It does not tell you though, which of the thousands of acceptable jobs, is the best one for you.

74

By exalting their human reason and common sense to such a high place of decision-making, these churchgoers are opening their lives to greater subjectivity than Christians who seek inner guidance from the Holy Spirit.

This greater subjectivity results from limiting one's major decisions to a human reason which makes mistakes and to a common sense which has been formed from the limited experiences of the fallible physical senses.

Problems of exalting human reason

An example of the enormous problems caused by over-exalting human reason and common sense relates to the question of whom to marry. By using reason and common sense to decide whom to specifically marry, often in a church, two young men find that they have both decided to try to marry the same girl.

Each young man says that his common sense and reason suggest that it is best that he marries the girl. This is subjective to the extreme!

A similar situation applies to jobs. By using limited common sense and reason alone, you could have 20 young Christians thinking that they were each most suited to one job in one specific firm. One could quote many similar examples.

Common sense and reason used correctly

The following example shows the correct place of common sense and human reasoning in a Christian's life. A Christian awakes to find her house on fire. Her husband and three children are still asleep.

In this situation, it would be foolish for this woman to spend half an hour or an hour asking the Lord what to do. By the time she would have finished praying, the house would be burnt down. She and her family would be burnt to death.

The correct thing to do instead would be for her to firstly

pray a two-second prayer, 'Lord, I'm trusting You to help and guide me." The next thing would be to use her common sense. Her common sense, because of her experience of fire in the past and hearing of the death experiences of other people who did not get out of a burning house, would tell her to awaken her family and get them outside as quickly as possible.

This is not an ungodly use of common sense.

While doing the above, if she would not be willing to have the Holy Spirit give her guidance, if He so desired, this would be a spiritually immature use of common sense. For God may see that the front door is jammed. If she tries to get her family out of the front door, they will get caught there and then be burnt alive.

God may wish to give her this information that her common sense and reason are not aware of. If she does not know how to recognize the Holy Spirit's voice or she is not willing to submit her common sense and reasoning to Him, she may indirectly cause them all to die.

You can use your God-given reason and common sense to make little decisions. However, always be ready to instantly ignore their advice, if the Spirit of Christ gives you inner guidance to do something which is opposite to what they suggest or understand. Also, never use them to make decisions contrary to the Scriptures.

The chapter, 'Day-to-Day Practise of Seeking God's Will', will expand on these matters.

Chapter 10   The God-given mind...what is it for?

1 Does God expect to use our God-given minds to decide where to live, who to marry and similar questions?
2 What is the mind of the flesh?

11

The human mind without God

The human mind or intellect is not an evil thing. This is because everything created by God is good. 1 Timothy 4:4 and Genesis 1:31 prove that every natural thing was originally created by Him as being good.

The problem though is that when Adam turned away from God, he lost the presence of the Spirit of Jesus in his mind, emotions, body and spirit. Romans 5:12 says:

Therefore as sin came into the world through one man and death as the result of sin, so death spread to all men (no one being able to stop it or escape its power) because all sinned.
Amplified Version

This verse says that all men died as a result of what Adam did.

Death is a result of a lack of life. Jesus said that He is 'the Life' in John 14:6. The Holy Spirit is the source of all life. Romans 8:2 and Revelation 11:11 both call the Holy Spirit the Spirit of Life. So Adam had a body which began to die and had a spirit that died in a spiritual sense, because the Holy Spirit no longer lived in and controlled his spirit, mind, emotions and body. The same thing happened to Eve.

And when they produced children, they produced children who didn't have God the Holy Spirit living in their spirits, minds, emotions and bodies. This is why all humans have tended to do wrong things since that time right up until today. Paul in Romans 8:6 brings out this point:

> **To be controlled by human nature results in death, to be controlled by the Spirit results in life and peace.**
> *Good News Version*

Romans 8:6 is talking about both the condition of a human's spirit and about the condition of a human's body. For a human spirit that is not indwelt by God the Father and God the Son in the Person of God the Holy Spirit is spiritually dead and will go to hell. This is what Jesus told the very religious man, Nicodemus, in John 3:5–6:

> **I am telling you the truth, that no one can enter the Kingdom of God unless he is born of water and the Spirit. A person is born physically of human parents, but is born spiritually of the Spirit.**
> *Good News Version*

Demons and Satan are examples of the result of rejecting the life, power and love of the Spirit of Christ. They are even more spiritually dead than humans who reject Jesus Christ and the power of the Spirit. Demons have been rejecting Him for thousands more years than many humans have.

Even though humans can allow God to make their spirits come alive (in the sense of being filled with Him), their bodies will still die. No Holy Spirit-controlled Christian is ever filled and controlled by Him enough in his body to reverse the dying process. Paul spoke of this in 2 Corinthians 4:16:

> **...though our outer man is progressively decaying and wasting away, yet our inner self is being progressively renewed day after day.**
> *Amplified Version*

As Romans 7:22–23 says, your inner self (your spirit), after you are born again of the Spirit, delights to obey God's teachings. However, your brain, emotions and body (referred to in verse 23 as your 'bodily members') tend towards wanting to sin.

The above explains why the human mind and emotions, even though they were originally created by God, are in a wrong state unless they are day by day given over to His Holy Spirit's control.

Even though the human mind is not evil in itself, it makes good decisions only if it's used the way the Maker made it to be used. He made it to be controlled by the presence and guidance of His Holy Spirit. Don't hate your mind and common sense. Keep them controlled by the Holy Spirit.

A human mind that is not controlled by the inner revelations and guidance of God the Holy Spirit is like a car without petrol or human emotions without love in them.

Chapter 11   The human mind without God

1 Is the human mind an evil thing?
2 Why is the human mind in a wrong state unless it is controlled by the presence and guidance of God the Holy Spirit?

12

The uncontrolled mind

The results of people not having their minds' reason and common sense submissive to God is seen firstly in the book of Judges. Judges 17:6 and Judges 21:25 say that at that time 'every man did what was right in his own eyes' – they did what their God-given minds thought was best.

Study the book of Judges and read what terrible backslidings away from God occurred among most people in Israel at that time.

Saul

King Saul is another example of someone doing what his God-given mind told him to do and getting into terrible trouble as a result. In 1 Samuel 15:1–29, we see that God told him to kill all of the demon-controlled wicked Amalekites and all of their animals. But Saul only obeyed part of what God said. He killed the Amalekites except their king. Also, he only killed some of the animals.

His God-given human mind told him that he should let his men keep the best animals for a sacrifice to God. But God wanted Saul to lovingly obey His guidance and not follow his own mind's decisions. Saul's human mind also thought that it would be good to allow the Amalekite king to be spared. Maybe, he thought that this would be a trophy. (Some churchgoers would probably do just as Saul did.)

But because he only partly obeyed God the Holy Spirit, God rejected him as King of Israel.

Joshua's major mistake

Even godly spiritual people can fall into the trap of allowing their human feelings and the so-called good reasoning and common sense of their human minds to lead them into disobedience to God.

Joshua and the people of Israel in Joshua 9:1–27 are an example of not seeking to discover the will of God. Instead, they followed the reasonings of their God-given human minds and followed what their God-given eyes and ears told them about the Gibeonites.

The Gibeonites belonged to a wicked demon-controlled idolatrous religion and were another group of the Canaanites, whom God told the Israelites to kill in Deuteronomy 20:16–18. To save their own lives, they dressed themselves and their donkeys in a way that would trick the God-given human minds of the Israelites. These Gibeonites dressed themselves in a way that made it appear to the Israelites' eyes and minds that they didn't come from Canaan. The Israelites didn't seek God's guidance about this matter. Joshua 9:14 says:

> **The men of Israel accepted some food from them, but did not consult the Lord about it.**
> *Good News Version*

These words in Joshua 9:14 reveal how much God wants our minds to depend and rely on His guidance and wisdom. Our mind must not rely on itself and on other humans' ideas.

This was the only time that Joshua didn't seek God's will in the Book of Joshua and trouble resulted. This is a tremendous lesson. Many churchgoers repeat this mistake of not seeking direction from God countless times.

As a result of following their human minds' reasonings

instead of the guidance of God, the Israelites couldn't destroy the demon-worshipping Gibeonites. This was tragic. The Gibeonites then lived as slaves amongst the Israelites and helped to lead many godly Israelites into evil religious practices in years later.

God wanted to help the Israelites avoid having this terrible problem. Because the Israelites relied on their human reasoning and common sense alone, trouble resulted.

The Apostle Peter's trust and reliance in his own mind

Another example of someone relying more on his own human mind's reasoning than on the wisdom and guidance of God is seen in the experience of Peter. When Jesus said that he was going to suffer much from religious leaders and be put to death (see Matthew 16:21–23), Peter tried to convince Jesus not to do this. Peter believed that it would be terrible for the Messiah to suffer and die in this way.

Peter, in this example, used his God-given mind to work out something that was against the will of God. Peter trusted more in his own plans in this instance than in Jesus' wisdom. Jesus told Peter that his thoughts came from man and not from God.

At another time in Peter's life, he caused himself trouble by relying too much on his own mind's wisdom again. Jesus told him that it was God's will that Peter could walk on water (see Matthew 14:22–32). Peter firstly trusted that Jesus would give him the power to walk on water. However, he then allowed his mind to concentrate on the waves and the strong winds. He probably began to concentrate on all of the things that his mind had ever experienced, been taught and had reasons. He probably thought, 'Humans don't walk on water', and 'Strong wind on the lake means danger', etc.

Once he started reasoning like this, instead of listening

to God the Son, he lost trust in God's power and wisdom. As a result, God's power stopped flowing. Remember Matthew 13:58 says that a lack of faith limits God's ability to perform miracles. If God limits His miracle-working to the amount of faith expressed in a person, who are we to argue with Him?

Verse 31 reveals that Jesus said that Peter began to sink when he doubted. His doubt came from listening to his mind instead of God's thoughts.

Another brilliant human plan that resulted in tragedy

Jeremiah 42 and 43:1−13 show an historical event where another group of people made their decisions on the basis of good human planning and reasoning and as a result disobeyed God.

At this time, the people of Judah asked Jeremiah to seek God's will for them. They promised that they would do God's will. This is seen in Jeremiah 42:5−6. At the end of waiting on Him for 10 days, God spoke to Jeremiah to tell the Jews to stop being afraid of the king of Babylon. God said that He would rescue them from the Babylonian king's power. Verses 7−12 reveal this.

However, because Egypt was a strong country far away from Babylon and seemingly strong enough to stand up to the Babylonian armies, most Judeans then used their God-given human minds to reason that it was safer in Egypt. They decided to go to Egypt (see Jeremiah 43:1−7).

God the Holy Spirit told them through the mouth of Jeremiah not to go to Egypt. (See Jeremiah 42:13−22.) However, they still went. They went because they trusted more in their human minds' abilities than they did in God's guidance. The Babylonians later conquered Egypt and the Judeans there died unnecessarily. They should have let their minds listen to the Lord instead of rejecting his guidance because it did not agree with their common sense and reasoning ability.

Ten spies who trusted in their limited human mind more than in God

Another example of religious people going by what their God-given human minds, eyes and ears told them, instead of by what God told them to do are the ten spies that Moses sent to look at the land of Canaan. In Numbers 13:27–29 and 31–33, these ten spies did what any human mind would do that wasn't desiring to listen to the wisdom of God.

They saw that the opposing soldiers were bigger than them, had very strong defences (including high walls around their cities) and had better weapons. They reasoned that God's promise that they would conquer these armies was false. They trusted more in their own minds' reasonings and common sense than in God's promises of victory found in Exodus 34:11. Many churchgoers today run their lives similarly to the proud human mind-dominated ten spies.

However, Caleb and Joshua ignored what their fleshly, human minds might have said and believed God's promise. This is seen in Numbers 13:30 and 14:6–9. Caleb and Joshua preferred to listen to and believe what God's Spirit told them. God was pleased with their attitude but not with the other spies' attitude (see Numbers 14:24, 30).

Are you like Caleb and Joshua? Or are you like the ten spies who were full of trust in their own reasonings and were full of doubts and unbelief as a result?

Pride is partly revealed where people have a self-reliant attitude in their own limited brains' abilities and where they do not depend and rely upon the Spirit of Jesus to control and fill their minds with His presence, wisdom and guidance (see Galatians 5:16 and 1 Corinthians 1:30). We can tell how much pride we have by seeing how self-reliant we are upon the natural abilities that God has given us. God never gave these abilities to be used without the help and presence of His Spirit filling and empowering these natural abilities.

Chapter 12   The uncontrolled mind

1 Why did Saul cause trouble for himself in the events spoken of 1 Samuel 15:1–29?

2 What does Joshua 9:14 reveal?

3 In the example quoted in Matthew 14:22–32, did Peter begin to sink because God decided, in the middle of miraculously helping Peter to walk on water, to no longer perform the miracle? Or was there another reason?

4 How many other examples in the scriptures can you find of people causing trouble for themselves because they decided to do something without seeking the guidance of the Spirit of Jesus?

13

Trusting in God's guidance

Here are good examples of how ridiculous it is to suggest that we should not spend much time seeking to know what God the Holy Spirit is telling us to do and that instead we should always follow what our God-given human minds tell us we should do.

In Joshua 6:3–5, we see that God told Joshua and his army to do some things which, to the human mind alone, would seem ridiculous. He told them to do the following:

> You and your soldiers are to march around the city once a day for six days. Seven priests, each carrying a trumpet, are to go in front of the Covenant Box. On the seventh day, you and your soldiers are to march around the city seven times while the priests blow the trumpets. Then they are to sound one long note. As soon as you hear it, all of the men are to give a loud shout and the city walls will collapse. Then the whole army will go straight into the city.
> *Good News Version*

When we read the above, we can imagine what the natural minds (which were not controlled by God) of the soldiers on the walls of Jericho would have been thinking? They would have probably laughed and thought, 'No army can conquer a city with high walls with these tactics. These Israelites are fools. Where are their ladders or battering rams? These people will never defeat us like this.'

86

Some of the Israelite soldiers may have been tempted to not allow the guidance of God to rule their minds. This would have led them to doubt that the walls by a miracle would collapse.

However, these Israelites, by the thousands, didn't doubt. Instead, they obeyed in faith what God told them to do. Because they didn't doubt that the walls would collapse, God destroyed the walls. God responded to the faith that was exercised by these Israelite soldiers in a promise spoken by Himself in Joshua 6:2–5.

This proven in Hebrews 11:30, which says:

It was faith that made the walls of Jericho fall down after the Israelites had marched around them for seven days.
Good News Version

The Israelite soldiers ignored what their reason and common sense told them. Instead, they were certain that the walls would fall down because God had promised that this would occur. As a result, God's Spirit moved in power to perform a miracle that He wanted to do.

If they had all doubted, God would have refused to have knocked the walls down. The effect of doubt is partially revealed by Matthew 17:19–20 and James 1:6–8 says:

But when you pray, you must believe and not doubt at all. Whoever doubts is like a wave in the sea that is driven and blown by the wind. A person like that, unable to make up his mind and undecided in all he does, must not think that he will receive anything of the Lord.
Good News Version

Babies being born through trust in God's guidance and power

Another example is seen in Genesis 15:4 and 17:1–19. Here, God told Abraham that his wife was going to have a son. There is nothing amazing about God telling someone that he/she is going to have a son. But when we consider that Romans 4:19 says that Abraham was almost 100 years old at the time, that his body was practically dead and that Sarah was past the age of child-bearing, then a God-given human mind that is not controlled by God the Holy Spirit would reason that to expect a child in such circumstances is ridiculous.

However, Abraham was always aiming to listen to what God wished to tell him. He didn't try to decide with his mind what was possible for himself. As a result, Sarah had a child at 90 years of age. (See Romans 4:16 – 22).

The example of Mary is another instance which shows how silly it is to believe that there is no need to submit our minds' reason and common sense over to the control of God's Spirit. For God in Luke 1:26–38 told Mary through an angel that she was going to become pregnant without ever having sexual intercourse with a man.

If Mary had tried to reason this out with her God-given human mind alone, she would have thought, 'This is ridiculous and unreasonable. No woman in history has ever had a baby without having sexual contact with a man'.

Mary's common sense and human reasoning would have rejected what the angel of God spoke to her if she had allowed her mind to rely on itself. Everything she had ever experienced with her five physical senses and everything her mind had ever been taught would have made what the will of God in her life was, seem impossible and absurd.

But because Mary allowed God the Holy Spirit to be the Lord and controller of her God-given mind, Mary was able to have faith for the impossible. And partly as a result of her reliance and dependence on God's guidance, God the Son entered a human body to be seen by the human race.

Let's be humble like Mary, Abraham, Joshua and others. Humility is allowing our human minds to be controlled by whatever the Spirit of Jesus tells us to do. It is pride to try to make our own decisions in life with minds and emotions not yielded daily to God the Holy Spirit. Proud churchgoers must change.

88

Chapter 13   Trusting in God's guidance

1   How could Joshua and his soldiers believe that they could defeat the people of Jericho by doing the seemingly foolish things that they were told to do in Joshua 6:3–5?

14

Be Holy Spirit-controlled

It is vital to let your mind be controlled by the Spirit of
God. According to the Word of God in Romans 8:5–6 and
Galatians 5:16, if you make your decisions in life solely on
the basis of what the reasonings of your human mind tell
you to do, and on the basis of how you feel emotionally
about various matters, you will be walking in the flesh. In
other words, you will be flesh-controlled.

The flesh is defined as 'the human mind, common
sense, emotions and will that are not under the control of
the Spirit of God'.

It is ridiculous to suggest that you are not flesh-controlled, if you are not under the control of God's Spirit.

A Spirit-controlled person, such as those mentioned in
Romans 8:5–6 and Galatians 5:16–25, is defined as a
person who allows his mind, emotions and body to be
controlled –

a) by the teachings of the Holy Scriptures,
b) by the inner witnesses of God the Holy Spirit in his
   spirit,
c) by the inner voice of God the Holy Spirit in his
   thoughts, and
d) on rare occasions, by dreams and so on, that come from
   God's Spirit.

If you are not controlled by these things, it is impossible

to be a Spirit-controlled Christian. For Galatians 5:16 shows, especially in the Amplified Version, that it is only those Christians who are responsive to and controlled by God the Holy Spirit, who do not live controlled by the flesh:

> But I say, walk and live habitually in the (Holy) Spirit – responsive to and controlled and guided by the Spirit, then you will certainly not gratify the cravings and desires of the flesh – of human nature without God.
> *Amplified Version*

Romans 8:6 speaks similarly to what Galatians 5:16 teaches. This is because, in the Amplified Version, Romans 8:6 clearly reveals that the human mind, including its reason and common sense, that is not controlled by the guidance and power of God the Holy Spirit will not achieve anything spiritually good when judged by God's standards. This verse says:

> Now the mind of the flesh which is sense and reason without the Holy Spirit) is death – death that comprises all of the miseries arising from sin; both here and hereafter. But the mind of the (Holy) Spirit is life and soul peace (both now and forever).

Note firstly that this verse says that a fleshly mind is defined as one that is not controlled by God's Spirit. So therefore, according to God, a mind that is not willing to instantly change direction or attitude if the Holy Spirit gives it inner guidance to do so, is a mind of the flesh.

In Galatians 5:19–21, God again says that the flesh can only decide to do things which are wrong. (Remember God's standards are far higher than human standards of goodness, e.g. God regards anger as being like murder. See Matthew 5:21–22). Romans 7:23 also says that the flesh by itself can do no good. So, the above stated conclusion from Romans 8:6 is clearly supported by other parts of Scripture.

Note that Romans 8:6 says that a mind which is not

every day yielded to the Holy Spirit and the teachings of His Scriptures, can only make decisions which don't result in spiritual life. This verse says that things of spiritual death (i.e. things not really based on God) will result from Christians not submitting their minds in the above way. Romans 8:6 says that things of spiritual death will not only result after death, but here and now as well.

Galatians 6:8 relates to the above also:

> For he who sows to his own flesh (lower nature, sensuality) will from the flesh reap decay and ruin and destruction, but he who sows to the Spirit will from the Spirit reap life eternal.
> *Amplified Version*

Churchgoers who don't allow their minds to be dominated by God the Holy Spirit's guidance, love and power, will surely reap decay, ruin and destruction in their spiritual lives.

Ungodly religious busyness

Much religious activity in the church at present is merely *the flesh busy doing a lot of things supposedly for Jesus*. Much evangelism, prayer meetings, building projects, teaching, school activity and so on, is not controlled by the Spirit of Jesus, but by fleshly minds. This is why so much effort at present in the church achieves very little. Galatians 6:8 predicted that this would happen.

Partly because of the lack of emphasis on obedience to the Holy Spirit (obedience is one aspect of being controlled by the Holy Spirit), there are thousands of people in the church at present who have not got their reason and common sense made subordinate to the Holy Spirit. They decide who to marry, where to live, how to run their church, what to teach their church members, who should help with the singing at church and so on. Instead, they should 'sow to the Holy Spirit' by allowing the Holy Spirit to show them what to do. Then as Romans 8:6 and Galatians 6:8 say, they will see spiritual life released from God into their lives and local congregations.

Much religious activity in the church is a great sowing to the flesh, which will reap decay, ruin and destruction for those churches and for those individual churchgoers who continue to do it. God in Galatians 6:8 said that this would happen. Meditate on this verse!

The example of the early church

God wants the Church to change back to how it was in the Book of Acts. There obviously was some sowing to the flesh in the time of the Book of Acts, but there was also in the time of Acts more sowing to the Spirit than occurs in many local churches now. Fantastic manifestations of God's power occured in the time of the Book of Acts, not only just in the lives of the church leaders. They also occured in the lives of thousands of ordinary church attenders.

These manifestations occurred partially because more people in the Church in those years day by day sought to know what the Holy Spirit wanted them to do and then they obeyed these instructions.

Revelation chapters 2 and 3 show that there was some sowing to the flesh in those days. Also, the comments made by Paul to the Galatian Christians, the Corinthian Christians, the Colossian Christians, the Philippian Christians, the Roman Christians and so on, show that some sowing to the flesh did occur in the early centuries. But the point to note is that the great expansion of the Church and the occurrence of many miracles of God show that there was more sowing to the Spirit in those times.

Some churchgoers are too apathetic or lazy to learn how to know when the Holy Spirit is speaking to them. This must change.

Other churchgoers are too proud, self-sufficient and independent of God, to want to know how to recognize the voice of God the Father and God the Son speaking to them in the Person of God the Holy Spirit. They don't want to learn because they want to be their own lord, even though they go to church and call Jesus 'Our Lord' or 'My Lord'.

Expect criticism

Many pastors and preachers, who preach the idea that the Holy Spirit must control our decision-making (which is the same as making Jesus as our Lord), will be persecuted by members of their own local congregation or their denomination who sow to a mind of the flesh. They must expect this if they preach as God would want them to. They should not let this worry them. This is because Jesus said in Matthew 5:10–11 that you are blessed when people, including churchgoers who sow to the flesh and are not controlled by the Holy Spirit, persecute you.

In fact, Paul said that all people who want to live a godly life in Christ Jesus must expect persecution (see 2 Timothy 3:12). Persecution includes great criticism and lies against oneself (see Matthew 5:10).

In fact, if you are a church leader and you are not being criticised, Jesus, in Luke 6:26, suggests that you are possibly no better than the false prophets. You had better check your spiritual life if unbelievers and fleshly churchgoers speak well of you. You are possibly not controlled by God very much (if at all).

Commands of God

Remember the following commands of God. God through the mouth of Paul said in Galatians 5:25:

> **If we live by the (Holy) Spirit, let us also walk by the Spirit – If by the Holy Spirit we have our life (in God), let us go forward walking in line, our conduct controlled by the Spirit.**
> *Amplified Version*

It is also very clear that God, in Romans 8:5–6 and

94

Galatians 5:16–24, commands us to be controlled by God the Holy Spirit. These are commands – Do we aim to obey them?

Being controlled by God's Spirit not only involves allowing ourselves to be controlled by the strength, power, Agape love and presence of God the Holy Spirit. It also involves being controlled by the wisdom of God found in the Holy Scriptures and by the inner guidance of His Holy Spirit.

Some people may argue against the importance of inner guidance from the Spirit of Jesus by saying that in the Book of Acts, we only see God giving inner guidance to Paul about eight times, to Peter about three times, and to Philip about one time and to Stephen about one time (see footnote). So they assume from this that God only on rare occasions gives inner guidance. They say that mostly He wants to use our minds' reasonings.

This is incorrect, because do we believe that the Spirit of Jesus only spoke to Paul by inner guidance eight times in his life, to Peter three times in his life, to Philip one time in his life and to Stephen one time in his life? Such a suggestion is nonsense. The correct thing is that the Book of Acts is a summary of the most important events in each of these people's lives. There were obviously hundreds of other times in their lives where the Holy Spirit gave them inner guidance. The fact that is a summary can be inferred from the comments made by the Apostle John in John 21:25 about his own gospel.

These other occasions of guidance would have never spoken contrary to Scripture.

Disobeying inner guidance

Disobedience to an inner voice and inner witness of God the Holy Spirit always causes trouble. For example, when I was working as a technical college teacher, I took more than the normal number of classes. I did this because one of my family kept encouraging me to earn as much money as possible. I took these extra classes without any guidance from God. I had no inner witness of peace or joy from His Spirit to do this.

As a result of this disobedience, I made myself so busy that I couldn't get enough sleep. I became irritable and tense because I was racing from one class to another. Also, I had resulting physical symptoms such as tight sick stomach and fast heart beat.

Another example of disobedience to God the Holy Spirit was where a number of years ago, God spoke by the inner voice a number of words into my thoughts telling me to warn a close Christian friend not to get involved with a girl who had just been converted. This girl wanted to become his girlfriend with the aim of possibly being engaged.

Many times as I prayed about this, I had an inner witness of peace about warning him. This friend was fairly strong spiritually but was a bit lonely at the time.

I disobeyed this inner voice and inner witness of the Holy Spirit because I allowed my human reasonings and human feelings to dominate me. I reasoned that he mightn't like me saying this to him. Also, I reasoned that it was none of my business. I also felt no peace in my emotions because of fear of trouble if I told him. This could have been mistaken for an inner witness.

I disobeyed God's inner voice and inner witness. This friend went with the girl. This girl encouraged him to not be as strong spiritually and after many months she backslid and caused my friend great heartache.

If I had obeyed, I might have saved him that trouble. It is possible that because we were friends, he may have sought God's will more deeply if I had told him what the Lord had spoken to me.

I had to confess this terrible disobedience. I owe my friend a lot because my disobedience caused him great trouble. May he, in love, forgive me.

It is better to obey the inner guidance of God the Holy Spirit, no matter what our feelings or human reasoning or common sense tell us or what other people's human reasoning or common sense tells us.

Lack of teaching on inner guidance

One of the biggest problems that prevents the church from being what God wants it to be is the fact that even though there is a good emphasis among many types of Christians on obedience to the teachings of the Bible, there is little understanding of the need day-by-day obedience to the inner guidance of the Holy Spirit. I have noticed this enormous problem amongst many Evangelical and Charismatic Renewal groups.

The lack of understanding of the need to obey constantly, hour by hour, the inner guidance of the Holy Spirit, leads many Evangelical and Pentecostal Christians to decide with their own minds things such as where to live, where to work, who to marry and other questions which are not specifically answered in the Bible. The Bible doesn't tell Anne to marry a person called Fred. It doesn't also tell a Christian called Peter to live in Peking.

The Bible only gives good general principles about these specific questions. The Bible tells you not to have jobs which involve stealing or murdering. But only the Holy Spirit could tell you by inner guidance which of the hundreds of jobs which don't involve stealing or murdering, is God's specific will for you.

As a result of so many Evangelical and Pentecostal Christians knowing not a lot about inner guidance of the Holy Spirit, there is much disobedience to God's will among thousands of even born-again Christians. Jesus is not the head of the body in many local churches. This is because so many born-again Christians don't know how to recognize the inner guidance of God the Holy Spirit.

Many of the hands, toes, legs, etc., of Jesus' body are doing what they want to do instead of what the head (that is, the Spirit of Jesus) (see Ephesians 4:16) is telling them to do. This makes the churches spiritually weak.

Chapter 14   Be Holy Spirit-controlled

1 What do Romans 8:5–6 and Galatians 5:16–25 teach about the difference between being Holy Spirit-controlled and being flesh-controlled? (Refer to Amplified Version if possible.)
2 Can a born-again Christian be very busy doing church activities, but still not be controlled much by the Holy Spirit?

Refer to Scriptures related to Paul (Acts 9:1–6, 13:2, 13:4, 16:6, 16:7, 19:21, 20:22, 27:10), Peter (Acts 4:8, 5:3, 10:19), Philip (Acts 8:29) and Stephen (Acts 6:10). In these Scriptural references, I have not included the few mentions of dreams, visions, and angelic appearances that occurred in these four men's lives, as recorded in summary in the Book of Acts.)

A number of people are seen in the Old Testament to have been guided by God. These people were not new creations in Christ, because they were not born-again of the Holy Spirit.

In New Testament times, millions of people are privileged to be born again of the Spirit of Christ. Because of this privilege, one could say that born-again Christians have a greater responsibility to be guided by the Holy Spirit than people in the Old Testament.

15

Seeking God's will daily

There is one problem which has been noted about trying to live a life of obedience to the inner guidance of the Spirit of Jesus. To live a life of loving obedience to God, do you have to pray for a long time about every one of the decisions that you have to make each day?

The following two sections will give the answer to this problem.

Big or medium sized decisions

Firstly, for things of big or medium sized importance, for instance which house you should live in, which town you should live in, which job you should have, where you should go on holidays, what things should you preach about in your sermon next week, which miracles are God's will for you to trust the Spirit of Jesus to perform for you (see Romans 8:26, Ephesians 6:18), should I allow my daughter to marry this man, should I play in a soccer competition this year, should I buy a new refrigerator or should I make do with the old one, and so on, you must spend time by yourself (if it is possible to find a place by yourself to pray where you live) in prayer seeking to hear the inner guidance of God the Holy Spirit.

If you do not do this, you are not aiming to be a Holy-Spirit-controlled Christian (Galatians 5:16, Romans 8:5–8). You are instead like the people in Joshua 9:14, who got themselves into a lot of trouble:

The men of Israel accepted some food from them but did not consult the Lord about it.
Good News Version

Smaller decisions

However, about smaller decisions, for instance, whether to have breakfast at 6.30 am or 8 am, whether to have four or six slices of bread for lunch, whether to go to the toilet now before I finished talking with my relative or to go after we have finished talking, whether to buy four cartons of fruit juice or none at all, whether to talk to my wife ten minutes or thirty minutes about a particular problem, whether to wash the clothes this morning or this afternoon or tomorrow, whether to go for a walk to the shops now or later, whether to wash the car with the hose or with water and bucket, and so on, you don't need to spend an hour in prayer waiting to hear God's Spirit give you guidance about what is His will for each of these decisions.

Proof of the fact that this is true is that in the Bible, you don't ever see anyone specifically waiting on God in prayer for an hour or so to see what His will was about these small things.

We can understand why God doesn't require us to wait on Him in prayer about these minor matters, because we make hundreds of small decisions every day. If we had to wait on God in prayer for an hour about every one of these decisions, we would have to spend more than one hundred hours each day waiting on God in prayer seeking His guidance. But since there are only twenty-four hours in each day and about eight hours of this is taken up by sleep, there would only be sixteen hours left each day for a Christian to use for this purpose. This is clearly not God's will.

We should not come into the bondage of trying to specifically pray about every one of the hundreds of little decisions that we have to make each day.

Basic guide about all decisions

God has a far better way for you to know what to do about these smaller decisions in life.

Firstly, He has given you His Scriptures to give you a basic guide of what is His will about many small decisions that you have to make each day. Therefore, if a small decision that you are considering making is opposite to the teachings of the Bible, you should let the Bible guide your decision making. If you are being asked by a boss at work to lie on a statistics sheet about the amount of work being done at the firm, you should obviously not lie.

You don't have to wait on God for an hour in prayer about this matter to see what God the Holy Spirit will give you inner guidance to do. This is because God the Holy Spirit would never give you inner guidance to do something that is the opposite of what He in the Holy Scriptures has already said.

Secondly, if the Scriptures do not give a clear answer as to whether one's proposed decision is God's will (for instance, should I eat tea at 5 pm or 6 pm? Should I clean my teeth before I wash my hands or after I wash my hands? Should I go 30 mph or 35 mph in my car? Should I read the newspaper for 10 minutes or 20 minutes?), one doesn't have to wait on God for an hour or so to find His will about each of these.

Instead, about these smaller matters, *continually* throughout the day, be aware of the presence of the Holy spirit and discern if you have an inner witness of peace or an inner witness of lack of peace, an inner voice or some other form of guidance. Be constantly, in an attitude of listening to the Holy Spirit. If the Spirit tells you to change your course of action then obey. Present your mind, body and spirit to God just as Romans 12:1 tells Christians to do'.

Having committed your mind, will and emotions to God the Holy Spirit, then believe He is guiding your thoughts, words and actions. This commitment is part of living a daily Spirit-filled, holy and obedient Christian life. Isaiah 30:21 infers this in part:

> **If wander off the road to the left or the right, you will hear his voice behind you saying 'Here is the road. Follow it'.**
> *Good News Version*

God has given you common sense and reasoning ability to decide what to do about these small matters. But as mentioned before, this common sense and reasoning ability should firstly never be allowed to lead you to decide to do anything contrary to the teachings of the Scriptures. Secondly, you should always be ready to ignore your common sense and reasoning if the Holy Spirit tells you to do something different from their advice.

You should constantly throughout the day on all occasions at work, at school, while shopping, and so on, be aware of the presence of the Holy Spirit. As a result, you will be allowing your mind and physical emotions to be controlled by the person, love, power and wisdom of the Spirit of Jesus.

God doesn't expect you to specifically spend half an hour or more each day seeking His Holy Spirit's guidance about when, where and how to clean your shoes or brush your teeth. However, He does expect you to be willing to listen if He does speak. You must learn how to recognize the inner still small voice (see 1 Kings 19:12) and inner witness (of peace or lack of peace) of His Holy Spirit so well that if He did happen to give you inner guidance just as you began to clean your shoes, that He wanted you to go and pray now for your mother, and then clean your shoes, you would be responsive enough to His Holy Spirit to allow the order of your actions to be changed. This is a part of being controlled by the Spirit of Jesus day by day, just as Romans 8:5–8 and Galatians 5:16 say.

Learn how to recognize the Holy Spirit's guidance and always have your mind willing and ready to receive guidance from God the Holy Spirit about these less important decisions. Otherwise, you can never properly live the sort of Holy Spirit-controlled, holy, dedicated-to-God life that all born-again sons and daughters of God should aim for.

Thirdly, when you have your specific periods of waiting on God in prayer each day (whether it is when you wake up and/or just before you go to bed and/or at some other time), you should not only seek to know His will about the more important things. You should also spend part of this time of private prayer in sincerely saying, 'Dear Spirit of Jesus, is there anything else that You want me to do in the day ahead, or week ahead, that You know that I haven't been seeking Your will about? If there is, I thank You that You will certainly give me guidance as to what it is, since You have promised to do so in James 1:5'. After making this commitment to God, you should then trust that His Spirit will surely speak to you during the rest of your prayer time and during the day anything else that He wants you to know.

This extra commitment to God's will will allow His Spirit to give you even more guidance of what He wants you to do at the times when you are busy at work or school and so on. At these times, you don't have hours to spare to listen to His voice.

In summary, there should be times each day when we set apart an hour or so to talk to and listen to Jesus Christ talk to us through the Person of God the Holy Spirit. But for the rest of the day, we should be constantly willing to have Him speak to us. This is even though we are not actively at these times spending an hour or so by ourselves where we do nothing but pray. Be aware of the presence of the Holy Spirit and conscious that having submitted our thoughts to him he will guide us in all we do.

An illustration

A comparison to the above is as follows: In an army, the sub-commanders find out what the General wants them to do in two main ways,

a) Firstly, there are times when the General gives an hour or more explanation of what the tactics for the battle are. At these times, the sub-commanders can ask him questions and have plenty of time to discuss what he wants them to do.

This is like in our Christian walk where we have our daily hour or so of continuous prayer each morning or each night, or at both of these times. At these times, we have plenty of time to talk to God and to listen to His guidance.

b) Secondly, while on the battlefield itself, the sub-commanders are too busy organising their soldiers and fighting the enemy (i.e. symbolic of demons and day to day problems), to go to talk with the general for an hour or more.

On these occasions, the sub-commanders must make quick decisions. They have not got time to go back to headquarters to talk for hours with the general. Nor have they got time to talk for hours on the radio with the general seeking to know what his will is.

Instead, on these occasions, the sub-commanders have to have the attitude that they are ready for the general to ring up on the radio at any time. The sub-commanders at these times cannot ring up the general to talk for an hour or so, because they are busy with leading their men and fighting the enemy. Therefore, they should always in a calm manner be ready for the phone from the general to ring.

This is just as you should be always ready for God to speak to you by His Spirit. This is while you do your work or go to school or do whatever else you have to do.

One final point that each Christian should realise from this comparison above is that the sub-commanders have to know what the sound of the radio or telephone is. This is because otherwise when the general rings, they won't even know that the general is calling them on the phone and that he is wanting to give them guidance and orders.

Similarly, unless you know how to recognize the inner guidance of God the Holy Spirit, Jesus may be ringing you up on His 'Holy Spirit spiritual telephone' and you may be totally unaware that He is trying to talk to you.

This is a sad thing which will cause you difficulty if this is true of your Christian life, just as it would cause great trouble for an army which operates without the sub-commanders knowing when the general is trying to ring them up.

Over a period of years, you must allow God to train you to be able to recognize when Jesus is trying to ring you on His 'Holy Spirit spiritual telephone'. Otherwise, you will always lead a weaker, less God-controlled Christian life.

Chapter 15   Seeking God's will daily

1 Should we specifically ask God what is His will about every one of the millions of decisions that we make each day? If not, what should we do?

2 Can Jesus be trying to speak to us by His Spirit and we not be aware of this? What sorts of things would cause us to be not aware that God is trying to speak to us?

16

Improving your ability to recognize God's voice

There are a number of key points about how to become more sensitive to the voice of the Lord Jesus Christ, speaking through the inner witness and the inner voice of the Holy Spirit. But firstly, it must be stated that these points are not a formula nor a list of mechanical religious exercises by which you can force Jesus to speak to you. These points are instead just things which should express in you a desire to hear Him speak to you regularly, because

a) you wish to love Him more deeply (Matthew 22: 34 – 38),

b) you wish to know Him in a more intimate and intensely personal way, and

c) you wish to love Him more than any other person or thing (see Matthew 6:33 and 10:37).

It is good to wish to know God's will and to obtain His solutions to your problems. However, these are not the main goals in seeking to more easily recognize His voice. The main goal is to personally love and know God more than before.

The importance of being willing to obey

The first important part of learning how to recognize the inner witness and the inner voice is you must become totally willing to do whatever God tells you to do. This is even if your human mind and emotions still tend to fight against you becoming like this. Only proud people think that they can run their lives better than what God the Holy Spirit could. God hates pride. James 4:6, 1 Peter 5:5–6 and Psalm 138:6 prove this.

An important reason why we don't hear God speak to us many times is this: Deep inside we don't want to obey. We say we do want to obey. However, deep within our mind and emotions, we only are willing to obey a certain few of the alternatives that God's Spirit may tell us to do. We must change ourselves with His Spirit's help in these areas of not being willing to obey 100%.

Some Christians do a similar foolish thing. They pray for guidance from God about a matter which He doesn't specifically reveal His will in Scripture, when they have already made up their minds about what they want to do or how they would like Him to answer. God will not guide such proud Christians. For example, a person may be praying about whether God wants him to be a church leader and because he has already decided to be one, God will not speak to him about it. He then disobeys foolishly.

Some Christians have to learn a lot of hard lessons before they are willing to obey God fully. Hebrews 12:7 – 11 proves this.

Don't have your mind made up already

People who pray for God's will, but have already deep in their minds decided what they want to do, often half-heartedly seek other advice. They visit many different church leaders until they find one who will agree with them that they should do what they have already decided to do. Then they will fool themselves by saying that this advisor is being used by God to tell them what His will is.

If you really have a 100% desire to do His will whatever it is, you will certainly have God the Holy Spirit speak to you His will. This is seen in Romans 12:1–2. These verses say that if you totally commit yourself in dedication to doing God's will, you will be able to find God's perfect and acceptable will for your life:

> So then, my brothers, because of God's great mercy to us I appeal to you. Offer yourselves as a living sacrifice to God, dedicated to His service and pleasing to Him. This is the true worship that you should offer. Do not conform yourselves to the standards of the world, but let God transform you inwardly by a complete change of mind.
> *Good News Version*

Then look at the result of this.

> Then you will be able to know the will of God – what is good and pleasing to Him and perfect.

These verses are joined with a 'then'. Therefore, if you don't do the first part, God won't show you His will very much, if at all.

John 7:17 says also that if you are a person who really desires to obey Him more than anything else (with no limits to what you will do if He tells you to do something), He will speak to you. This verse says:

> If any man desires to do His will (God's pleasure), he will know – have the needed illumination to recognize, can tell for himself – whether the teaching is from God or whether I am speaking from Myself and of My own accord and of My own authority.
> *Amplified Version*

Not offering God a choice

Some Christians come to God and foolishly say things such as, 'Which of these two towns do you want me to live in, Lord?' They forget that seeking God's guidance involves having the attitude of being willing to live in any one of the millions of towns, villages and cities in any of the hundreds of countries in the world at the present time. Getting guidance doesn't involve giving Him a limited number of alternatives that you will obey.

One writer expressed the correct attitude. He said, 'The first step is to put myself in neutral gear – not forward or backward, but completely calm in my heart. Then I wait upon the Lord, saying, 'Lord, I'm here. I will listen to Your voice. If You say 'yes', I will go; if You say 'no', I'm not going. I don't wish to make decisions for my own benefit, but to decide according to Your desire.'

Don't seek in prayer to have God speak to you His will about something that He has already revealed in the Holy Scriptures. For example, don't pray that the nice young Christian man who is already married will leave his Christian wife to marry you. For the Holy Scriptures say that adultery is sin.

Only seek inner witnesses and inner voices about matters which the Holy Scriptures don't give specific answers – for example, about whether God wants you to live in France or Africa or somewhere else.

Express love to God in words

The second thing you must do to improve your ability to recognize God the Holy Spirit's voice, is expressing love to Him. Every day, often in your words and thoughts, praise God, thank Him and tell Him how much you love Him.

The Psalms are full of the evidence that He wants you to do this. Study the Psalms to check that what I'm saying is right. (Don't just believe what I am telling you is true. Check to see if what I'm writing is based on the Holy Scriptures.)

Acts 13:2 shows that God the Holy Spirit will more readily speak when Christians are praising, worshipping and telling God in their words and thoughts how much they love Him:

> **While they were worshipping the Lord and fasting, the Holy Spirit said ...**
> *Amplified Version*

One way of doing the above is firstly to lie on your back or sit down in a comfortable position where your mind will not be distracted by any noise. While doing this, tell God that you are willing to do whatever He says.

Remember that God will never tell you to do something that isn't really good for you in the long run. This is because He is the only totally loving unselfish being who exists. Even when He allows a bit of trouble in your life, it is only because He sees that it will help you grow to be more unselfish and spiritually mature than what you were before.

After making this obedience commitment, you should then begin saying over and over again things such as, 'Praise God', 'Bless God', 'I Love You Lord', 'Thank You for guiding me', 'Thank You for taking control of my life by Your Holy Spirit', 'Thank You for not allowing me to be misled by my own silly human plans or by thoughts that demons put into my mind', and similar expressions that are based on Bible principles. (See 2 Chronicles 20:21–23, Psalms 135, 136, 138, 145 to 150 and James 1:5–8.)

You should be careful not to do this like the heathen religions would. Jesus in Matthew 6:7–8 warns that a true Christian should not just repeat the same phrases over and over again in an empty way.

Instead, say these things with the aim of deepening the expression of love in your heart for God.

Remember that by saying these things to God you are not earning an answer from Him. Nor will saying these things force Him to speak to you. Instead, your goal in saying these things is to help intensify and deepen your personal relationship to Him. The more you deepen your communion with Him, the more easily you will be able to recognize His Spirit's voice.

Say these things in praise and worship for more than just five minutes. It is rare for God's Spirit to speak to you, until you have had enough time to get your mind and emotions quiet enough to hear the inner voice of God the

Holy Spirit or to be able to recognize His inner witness in your human spirit.

Sometimes, you have to pray like this for long periods before you will recognize God speaking to your mind.

The following point is sometimes neglected though when Christians discuss what good praise and worship is. Romans 12.1 says that making a total dedication of yourself to being willing to obey whatever God may tell you to do, is a part of spiritual worship. So for Jesus to speak to you by God the Holy Spirit while you are worshipping, you will have to totally rid your mind of any tendency to not want to obey whatever he may be going to tell you to do.

Ask God to teach you

The third important part of learning to be sensitive to the inner witness and inner voice of God the Holy Spirit is to, day by day, ask God to teach you what inner guidance really is. John 14:26 says that the Holy Spirit will teach you about everything. Therefore, God is seen to be clearly willing to teach you what inner guidance is.

You will not understand the inner witness and the inner voice if you try to work them out with your human mind without the revelation of the Holy Spirit of God. 1 Corinthians 2:14 shows this. This verse says indirectly that the natural mind doesn't understand the things of God.

Wait on God often in prayer

The fourth key in learning to be sensitive to the inner guidance of the Spirit of Jesus is that you must learn to spend a lot of time waiting on God in prayer (see Psalm 25:5). The people who know His will most and are most sensitive to the voice of His Holy Spirit, are those who spend a lot of time in prayer.

As stated earlier in this chapter, the amount of time that you pray doesn't force God to speak to you, or earn you an answer from Him. A lot of prayer, however, helps to strengthen your communion with God. As a result, you will be able to recognize more clearly when He is speaking to you.

Wesley was greatly led by the Spirit of Christ. He used to spend at least one hour every morning and at least one hour every night in prayer. Finney used to be led greatly by Jesus Christ through the person of His Holy Spirit. He used to at times spend four hours each morning talking to and listening to his Heavenly Father. Whitefield was very sensitive to God's Spirit and used to spend hours each day in prayer. Goforth, who spread by God's power great spiritual renewal in China in the early 1900's, spent hours in prayer each day and as a result came to know the inner guidance of His Holy Spirit greatly.

These men tried to obey the Bible command of praying without ceasing (see 1 Thessalonians 5:17) and the Bible command of being led by the Holy Spirit (see Romans 8:14, Galatians 5:25). As a result, they achieved fantastic spiritual results for the church of Jesus Christ.

There will always be something lacking in your Christian life if you don't come into realm of being led by God the Holy Spirit through the inner witness of peace and joy and through His voice in your thoughts.

But once again, remember that these forms of guidance never will lead you to do something contrary to the teachings of the Bible. The Bible has greater authority than these secondary types of guidance.

Don't doubt

James 1:5 expresses a tremendous promise which reveals that God wishes to guide and speak to us all. It says:

> **But if any of you lacks wisdom, he should pray to God, who will give it to him; because God gives generously and graciously to all.**
> *Good News Version*

However, if you ask God for guidance and it doesn't come straight away, don't begin to doubt that God will guide you. If you do doubt, this will prevent God the Father from revealing His will to you through His Holy Spirit. James 1:6–8 are verses which prove this fact since they relate to the promise in James 1:5. They say:

> **But when you pray, you must believe and not doubt at all. Whoever doubts is like a wave in the sea that is driven and blown about by the wind. A person like that, unable to make up his mind and undecided in all he does, must not think that he will receive anything from the Lord.**
> *Good News Version*

I have known of Christians seeking God's will for an hour or so and still not receiving guidance and then beginning to doubt that God would guide them. They then failed to receive any guidance at all.

Don't accuse God of lying when He promised to guide you by His Holy Spirit, by firstly trusting Him to reveal His will to you and then an hour or a day later doubting that He will do so.

Matthew 13:58 shows that God in His Sovereign Will has decided in many circumstances to limit miracle-working manifestations of His Holy Spirit's power to whether a human responds with faith in His promises in the Bible or in the Words of the Lord spoken directly by His Holy Spirit to the person. This verse says:

> **And he did not many miracles there because of their lack of faith.**

This verse doesn't say that Jesus decided not to do many miracles there, because He didn't want to perform miracles there. Instead, this verse shows that God in his own mighty sovereign will required faith responses from the people of Nazareth to the Words of the Lord that were spoken by Jesus on the day referred to in Matthew 13:58, before He would perform miracles.

Remember that Hebrews 11:1 says that a faith attitude is where you are certain or sure that what God promises in His Bible or through the inner guidance of His Spirit, will come to pass. Therefore, doubting is where you are uncertain that God will do what He has promised.

Who are we to argue with God, if He has decided to limit His power on many (but not all) occasions to humans using their gift of faith (which originally was given to them by Him) in an act of complete trust that His individual Word or promise to them will come true?

No human can limit God's power. Only God Himself could decide to limit His power on some occasions to a faith response (attitude of certainty) from a human.

If you find it hard to believe that God in many instances limits his manifestation of power and miracles to a faith response, look at Matthew 13:58 again. God says in this verse the words, '*Because* of their lack of faith'.

If you think that this is taking a scripture out of context, then consider Hebrews Chapter 11. In this chapter, God said that it was by faith that miracles occurred in the Old Testament times.

Faith is a gift of God according to Galatians 5:22, Ephesians 2:8 and Romans 12:3. However, it is a gift that must be put into practise by a Christian or it is useless.

When a person is converted, after hearing and receiving God's Word about Jesus Christ, the Holy Spirit gives him the gift of faith. This is seen in Romans 10:17. He also has free will and therefore the freedom to decide whether he is going to make use of this gift of faith from God.

The gift of faith never leaves the person. This is because the Holy Spirit doesn't leave a Christian, unless he totally turns away from God. Since faith is a fruit of the Holy Spirit as Galatians 5:22 says, this gift of faith is always in a person who has the Holy Spirit in him.

If a Christian doesn't put his faith into action he cannot blame God. Since God has given the Christian in his born-again experience the gift of faith and also free will that enables him to obey God and exercise this gift of faith, then the Christian is himself responsible before God if he doesn't use this God-given ability. Hebrews 11:6 confirms this where it says:

But without faith it is impossible to please and be satis-factory to Him.
Amplified Version

James 2:17–26 shows that this faith must be put into action and used by the Christian, otherwise his God-given gift of faith is dead and useless.

Faith cannot be worked up by our own human efforts (see Ephesians 2:8). However, because faith is a result of the action of the Holy Spirit and the Word of God, if we refuse to exercise this gift of faith once we have it, we are responsible.

Listen, obey, confess and turn away from sin

The sixth key to becoming more sensitive to God's Spirit's voice is that you must learn (a) to constantly obey the teachings of the Scriptures, the inner witness and inner voice of God the Holy Spirit and (b) to daily confess and turn away from any sin.

If you are disobedient to the Scriptures and of God the Holy Spirit in your spirit and His inner voice in your thoughts then eventually you will find difficulty in discerning what is from God and what is from Satan. You will also find that He will not be willing to guide you in these realms as much as he would a person who is more obedient to His Holy Spirit.

Moses, Joshua, David, Paul, Peter, Whitefield, Torrey, Studd, Moody, Finney and others were led by the Holy Spirit more than other people because they were more willing to obey and be led by the Holy Spirit than others. (See Galatians 5:18 and Romans 8:14.)

If you do fall into disobedience, you should immediately

confess your sin to God and ask His forgiveness. You should do as 1 John 1:9 says:

> **If we confess our sins, He is faithful and just to forgive us our sins, and to cleanse us from all unrighteousness.**
> *Authorized Version*

By doing this, you will remove any blocks that the sin may create in your communication and communion with God.

Praying in the Spirit

The seventh key which helps a person become more sensitive to the inner witness and inner voice of the Holy Spirit is praying in the Spirit often. God through the words of the Apostle Paul in Ephesians 6:18 spoke of this:

> **Pray at all times – on every occasion, in every season – in the Spirit, with all (manner of) prayer and entreaty...**
> *Amplified Version*

This is a command of God. Do you intend to obey it? Jude 20 also talks of praying in the Holy Spirit:

> **But you, beloved, build yourselves up (founded) on your most holy faith – make progress, rise like an edifice higher and higher – praying in the Holy Spirit.**
> *Amplified Version*

When I have prayed for an hour or more in the Holy Spirit, I found that my mind could far more easily recognize God's voice. I've prayed in the Spirit alone for five to six hours on some days. Usually, all other things being equal, the longer you pray in the Spirit on a particular day, the more sensitive you will become to God's voice.

Praying in the Spirit involves allowing the Spirit to inspire your words as you pray. Trust the Lord to give you the ability to pray in the Spirit.

Just because you have not possibly experienced praying

in the Spirit, don't let your experience encourage you to reject the above commands of Scripture. Sadly, some church leaders reject the above Scriptural commands, because their religious experiences tell them that praying in the Spirit does not occur these days. They teach experience-based doctrines and not Scripture-based doctrines about these things.

Don't give up because of mistakes

The eighth and final point about becoming more sensitive to God's inner guidance is that you must put up with the fact that you will at first possibly make a number of mistakes about this type of guidance from Him. You will sometimes possibly mistake your own human feelings or human emotions of joy and peace for the inner witness of joy and peace from His Holy Spirit. You will also possibly mistake your own human thoughts for the inner voice of His Holy Spirit sometimes.

In the first five or so years that I was learning how to recognize the voice of His Holy Spirit, I made many mistakes. I thought that God was leading me to be an intercessory partner with a fellow Christian, when He was not. I also wrongly thought that God's Spirit was leading me to write to an American Bible teacher to ask him to ask God for guidance for me. The fellow wrote back virtually suggesting that I get guidance from Him myself.

I wrongly thought that God was guiding me by an inner peace to get an Arabic friend to teach me Arabic. I also wrongly believed that I was meant to live with a particular family while I was teaching in Sydney, when I was not. I could give you other examples also.

I make far fewer mistakes in recognizing the voice of the Holy Spirit these days. But just like all limited human beings, I still have to test my so-called 'guidance' in order to avoid more mistakes.

Don't give up after a few mistakes! Just as a child has to gradually learn how to read and write and will make mistakes while learning to do so, so you will possibly make mistakes in this. God will be happy with you if you are at least trying constantly to lean how to communicate with Him more deeply.

Jesus will only be sad with you if:

a) you don't bother trying to learn, or
b) you give up after making a few mistakes in recognizing the joy and peace of the Holy Spirit or the inner voice of His Spirit as the second or third most important means after the Scriptures by which He speaks to us.

Even though you will possibly make mistakes in recognizing the voice of the Holy Spirit, do not wrongly think that it is very hard to learn how to recognize His voice. More than any one else, God wishes to communicate intimately with you. Therefore, He will never make becoming sensitive to the voice of His Spirit too difficult for you to learn.

Some Christians are so afraid of making a mistake in recognizing His Holy Spirit's voice, that they never mature in these matters.

Chapter 16
Improving your ability to recognize God's voice

1 We can't earn guidance from God. Also, we can't force God to speak to us. However, how can we become more receptive to when Jesus is speaking to us by His Spirit?
2 What does James 1:5–8 reveal about the importance of being sure that God will guide us?

17

Godly counsel

Another thing which helps you to discern God's voice is seeking the advice of godly types of church leaders. Sometimes, by sharing with you some unfamiliar parts of the Holy Scriptures, they can help you to learn to recognize God's voice. Proverbs 23:12 says:

> **Apply your mind to instruction and correction and your ears to the words of knowledge.**
> *Amplified Version*

Whether you are a church leader or a lay-person, you must be humble enough to sometimes seek the advice of other church leaders. One way that Satan can deceive you is to tempt you to never be willing to accept spiritual advice from church leaders.

Satan can lead you into what outwardly appears to be a 'total dependence on Jesus and the Spirit's guidance', but is really only another form of spiritual immaturity.

Some people falsely think that 'total dependence on Jesus' involves 'Jesus and me and no one else'. They forget that God has put ministers in the church to give advice, counsel, teaching and encouragement to all lay people and to other ministers. Ephesians 4:11–12 says:

> **And He gave some, apostles; and some prophets; and some evangelists; and some pastors and teachers; For**

the perfecting of the saints, for the work of the ministry, for the edifying of the body of Christ.
Authorized Version

It is dangerous for a Christian in so-called 'humility and obedience to God' to separate himself from all local churches and to aim to be a Christian by himself. He is an easy target for Satan if he does this. Satan can trick a person into thinking that he is humble, when he is in fact proud, self-reliant and unteachable.

The author has sadly known of people who have boldly claimed that God told them to do something. They said that it was a 'Thus says the Lord' which they had to obey. However, these individuals were really only covering up their own unscriptural desires and self-dependence, by imagining that God had told them to do what they disobediently had wanted to do in the first place.

It is very difficult to help such people, because Satan has deceived them into thinking that they are so humbly reliant on and obedient to God.

The above is one extreme. The other extreme are those who are spiritually immature in the fact that they are always looking for ministry and to Christian friends to guide them in most of their decisions. Such people usually waste days of their church leaders' time. They ignore the need to find God's will through Scripture study and an intimate prayer relationship.

Trust the Lord to reveal to you if you are at present trapped in either of these errors. God does not wish you to be caught in either of these extremes.

Every person (including all ministers) needs to be humbly open to receive advice and ministry from other church leaders. However, this does not mean that they should regard their counsel as infallible.

Remember that all humans can make mistakes. Therefore, always test all advice, 'revelations', 'prophecies' and teachings that a church leader gives you. (See 1 Thessalonians 5:21). Test them by the two methods outlined in the chapter 'Test all things'. If you don't, you could be misled by their mistakes. Some Christians have been led into great error by not testing the advice given to them by various ministries.

Be careful though not to judge their advice in terms of your own possibly false understanding of certain parts of the Scriptures. Be humble enough to see if your own understanding of the Scriptures related to whatever advice they are giving, is correct, partly correct or even false.

Take care when choosing who to counsel you. Firstly, make sure that the leader is born-again. If he is not, he will give you ungodly advice. Choose a person whose life expresses the fruit of the Holy Spirit such as patience, kindness, unselfishness, humility and peacefulness (see Galatians 5:22). Look for someone who aims to be very trusting and dependent on God and His Spirit within him. Seek for someone who aims to be more and more obedient to the Holy Scriptures' teachings. Avoid someone who talks and thinks about himself too much and who is proud and self-reliant.

Remember that spiritual maturity only in some cases comes in proportion to one's years as a church leader. Some church leaders have studied theology for forty to fifty years, but still do not know God.

Be open to counsel and advice from your spiritual leaders. Prayerfully and humbly consider their advice and test it by the Scriptures.

Chapter 17   Godly counsel

1 What are the advantages in seeking counsel from church leaders?
2 What dangers are there to avoid in seeking advice from others?

18

Extra points to note

No reasons given

Another point to note is that many times when God guides
you to do something by an inner witness, an inner voice, a
dream or by some other supernatural means, He will at
the same time give you reasons why He wants you to do
this. However, at other times, He will guide you to do
something without telling you any of the reasons.

I faced this situation a while ago. I was offered a teaching position at a good Christian private high school.

It was a better paid job than one that I had at the time.
It was a school where I liked to teach the Bible. At this
school, I would have been working with other good Christians. There were many other good features about this
school. My human reason and common sense after hours
of thought told me to take the job.

However, after two or three hours of talking to God and
trying to listen to His voice, the following occurred. Every
time I would picture in my mind teaching in this school's
classrooms, I would get a tight uneasy lack of peace in my
spirit.

Then when I would picture not working at this school, I
would get a tremendous peace and joy in my spirit. This
was even though my brain's reason and common sense
were saying that it was best that I take the job.

I obeyed the inner witness of the Holy Spirit. This was

even though at the time, God would not tell me even one reason why He did not want me to take the job. He wanted me to learn to obey His voice without knowing any good reason why I should take this action.

The main reason why the Spirit of Jesus sometimes will guide you to do something but will not tell you any reasons why He wants you to do this thing is that He is trying to teach your mind to not be so self-reliant. He wants your mind to be more and more controlled and filled by Himself.

Your mind has to stop being so reliant on its own reasoning ability and common sense, by being willing to do something which God's Spirit tells it to do, when it doesn't know one good reason why it should obey this guidance. This will result in your mind becoming more reliant on and controlled by the Spirit of Jesus. Your mind will then be obeying God's commands in Galatians 5:16, 5:25 and Romans 8:5–8.

It was only about five weeks after I told the Christian school's principal that it was not God's will that I take the job, that God showed my why He didn't want me to take the job. This was an important lesson for me.

Remember Joshua and Abraham

One example in the Holy Scripture of believers being guided by God to do something without God telling them any reason is seen in the previously quoted example of Joshua 6:2–5. Here God told Joshua and his soldiers to do some things for seven days, which seemed to have no good natural reason. Read these verses!

God told Joshua and his soldiers to do these things (which had no good human military tactical basis to them) in order to encourage these men not to rely on their limited human reasoning and common sense. God wanted them to die to self-reliance (see 2 Corinthians 4:10 and 12:9–10) and instead, to begin to have God-controlled minds (see Galatians 5:16, Romans 8:5–8), by obeying Holy Spirit guidance without having any natural understanding of why they should do such things.

Abraham had to face similar situations. He had to face the situation where God had not given him a child while he and Sarah were physically capable of this but where God later decided to give him a child when he and Sarah were physically too old to have a child (see Genesis chapters 12–21). He was then told to sacrifice his son (see Genesis 22).

In each of these circumstances, Abraham had no knowledge given by God to him of why God wanted these events to occur in these ways. As Proverbs 3:5 says, Abraham had to trust in the Lord and not rely on his own knowledge, reasoning and common sense.

What would you do in similar circumstances?

Angels, visions, dreams and audible voices

We see in the Book of Acts and elsewhere in the Bible how God led believers. At times, some received guidance through a vision, a dream or an audible voice. Others received guidance from an angel who appeared and told them what to do. Such phenomena however, did not happen every day in these people's lives. They occurred once or twice in a lifetime in most cases. So these are not the main ways that God speaks.

If you look at the lives of people in the Bible, you will never observe them seeking a vision or dream or an audible voice or a visit from an angel. However, you will find that when they did have these things, they didn't reject them. (See Matthew 2:12, 2:13–14, 2:19–21, 2:22, Luke 1:11–22, 1:26–38, 2:9–20, Acts 1:10–11, 9:3–7, 10:9–48, 16:9–12 and many others.)

However you must be very careful. This is because demons can imitate angels. See Galatians 1:8 and also 2 Corinthians 11:14 which says:

> **Even Satan can disguise himself to look like an angel of light.**
> *Good News Version*

You should also note that you can have dreams which are merely a product of what you have been thinking about in previous days. Also, you can have a nightmare through eating too much just before going to bed.

You should also note that demons can pretend to be God speaking with an audible voice.

Also, note that not all visions are from God. People saying that they had visions from God when they really didn't are seen in Colossians 2:18. Some false visions are a result of Satanic miracles (see Matthew 24:24, Revelation 16:14). Others are a result of men imagining these things or of lying that they have had visions from God when they had not (see Deuteronomy 18:21–22, Jeremiah 14:14, 23:16).

Never try to force God to give you a vision or to send an angel to you or to speak to you in a voice that can be heard by your physical ears! If you try to force God to speak to you in these ways, a demon might see what you are doing and then try to trick you, by imitating God's audible voice, or by pretending to be an angel or by giving you a psychic-witchcraft type of vision. If however, you do have one that you think is from God, test it (see 1 Thessalonians 5:21) to see if it is in agreement with the teachings of the Scriptures.

God guides step by step

When God guides us, He usually does it step by step. He mostly tells us what He wants us to do next, after we have obeyed the previous directions of His Holy Spirit. God doesn't tell us all that is going to happen in the future. God does this so we may not feel that we can live our lives without every day getting guidance from His Spirit. This encourages us to see how absolutely necessary it is each day to rely more and more on His Spirit within us.

An illustration of this is Paul in Acts 16:6–10. Here, Paul and Silas were firstly told by the Holy Spirit not to go to Asia. They then tried to go into Bithynia. However, the

HOW TO RECOGNIZE GOD'S VOICE

Spirit of Jesus revealed to them that this wasn't God's will (verses 7–8). Then God revealed in a dream that Paul had to go to Macedonia. Paul and Silas obeyed each of these steps. The point to note is that Paul went to Macedonia, not knowing that he would cast out a demon, end up in a terrible prison, have God help him escape by sending an earthquake and then see the jailer and his family converted to Jesus. God leads step by step.

Other reasons why God leads step by step are these. Firstly, if we knew all of the future, we would become proud of the good things that will happen to us. Secondly, if we knew a lot of the future, we would possibly become fearful of all the troubles and tragedies that will happen in our lives.

Rely totally on God

Getting guidance from God is like the time I was at Towradgi Beach in Wollongong in Australia. While I was swimming, I was caught in a deadly rip and began heading out to sea. I wasn't a good enough swimmer to be able to swim back to shore.

So as I was heading out to sea, I had to pray as I was treading water, 'Lord, I commit myself totally into Your hands. I am willing to do whatever You tell me to do in this circumstance'. Are you at this point of committal? Sometimes, I slip out of this level of commitment, but I always aim to return to this same level of willingness to obey.

As I was getting a long way off the shore, I said to God, 'I can't die Lord, because Your Spirit has told me previously that You still have many things that You want me to do before I die'. God's Spirit had spoken in the years prior to this event, many things that hadn't been fulfilled in my life by that time. So, I had a number of words of the Lord on which I could exercise faith that I wouldn't die. For remember, that you can only exercise faith and be sure that your prayer will be answered if you have a word of the Lord to base your prayer on (see Romans 10:17).

I refused to fear, even though I was greatly tempted by it. Fear is one of the opposites of faith and trust in God (Matthew 8:26), Mark 4:40, Luke 8:50 and Matthew 14:30–31. So God had a young friend come out on a surfboard and save me.

We need to often get to the place of nearly dying before we will be willing to obey God more. At this greater level of commitment, we will see God's power and Holy Spirit more evident in our mind, emotions and life.

Chapter 18   Extra points to note

1   Look for a number of examples in the Scriptures of believers being told to do something without God telling them any reason why He wanted them to do the thing:
2   Look for examples in the Scriptures of God guiding a person, step by step.

Some Christians I've met do not know the difference between a vision and a mental picture created in our minds by the inner voice of the Holy Spirit. I can speak to you the word 'dog' and most likely this will create a mental picture of a dog in your mind. Similarly God can speak to you. For example, the word 'shield' by the inner voice and this will most likely create a mental picture of a shield in your mind. This is very different to a vision. Visions are far more spectacular.

Mental pictures created by the inner voice of the Holy Spirit are far more common than visions.

The English word 'vision' has a number of meanings. It can mean 'an aim' or 'a goal'. It can also refer to 'a mental picture created by our minds'—this being different from a mental picture created through God speaking to us by the inner voice. Further confusion about what visions are, results from some Christian books defining the word 'vision' in one way and other books defining it in other ways.

What Devotion to God and Holiness Is Not

To understand what devotion to God and holiness is, is to know what it is not. This book reveals many teachings and practices in relation to devotion to God that have been wrongly accepted by large numbers of churchgoers over the centuries, even though these were contrary to the teachings of God's Holy Scriptures. This writing traces the sources of many of these ideas to the teachings of Hindus and Buddhists about holiness – ideas so deceitfully attractive to some that they could be mistaken for Christian teachings.

By reading this book, we can see if any of our present problems are a result of our unknowingly still clinging onto such false ideas and practices.

Highest Authority...Church, Scripture or Tradition?

This book examines in detail a question that relates to every Christian denomination. This question is: which is God's highest authority in our lives: the Church, the traditions of the Church or the Scriptures?

This is a very important question. We must be sure we know the correct answer. Our salvation, and the depth of our personal relationship with God, depends in part on how we answer this question and then how we use this knowledge.

*For a full list of SOVEREIGN WORLD international books
please write to:*

P.O. Box 17, Chichester, England
P.O. Box 329, Manly, N.S.W. 2095, Australia
P.O. Box 24086, Royal Oak, Auckland, New Zealand
14 Balmoral Road, Singapore 105